Merja Paksuniemi

The Historical Background of School System and Teacher Image in Finland

Bibliographic Information published by the Deutsche Nationalbibliothek
The Deutsche Nationalbibliothek lists this publication in the Deutsche Nationalbibliografie; detailed bibliographic data is available in the internet at http://dnb.d-nb.de.

Cover image:
Students at the teaching practise
at the Training school in 1934. OMA, TSeA, Ia.
Printed by courtesy of the Archive of Oulu.

Library of Congress Cataloging-in-Publication Data

Paksuniemi, Merja.
 The historical background of school system and teacher image in Finland / Merja Paksuniemi.
   pages cm
 ISBN 978-3-631-64310-5
 1. Schools—Public relations—Finland. 2. Teachers—Finland—Public opinion. I. Title.
 LA1011.P35 2013
 370.94897—dc23
                                                            2013020990

ISBN 978-3-631-64310-5 (Print)
E-ISBN 978-3-653-03235-2 (E-Book)
DOI 10.3726/978-3-653-03235-2

© Peter Lang GmbH
Internationaler Verlag der Wissenschaften
Frankfurt am Main 2013
All rights reserved.
Peter Lang Edition is an Imprint of Peter Lang GmbH.

Peter Lang – Frankfurt am Main · Bern · Bruxelles · New York ·
Oxford · Warszawa · Wien

All parts of this publication are protected by copyright. Any utilisation outside the strict limits of the copyright law, without the permission of the publisher, is forbidden and liable to prosecution. This applies in particular to reproductions, translations, microfilming, and storage and processing in electronic retrieval systems.

www.peterlang.de

I would like to thank the University of Lapland
for supporting my research.

Contents

1. Introduction 9

2. Theoretical starting points 11
   2.1. The Finnish teacher image–requirements and changes 11
   2.2. Teacher training, professional development and maturity 17
   2.3. The teacher image 22
   2.4. Method of research and source material 24

3. At the roots of the Finnish school system 27
   3.1. Aiming to produce educated citizens for society 27
   3.2. Christianity and decency through discipline and order 29
   3.3. The development of compulsory education 33

4. Teacher training colleges in Finland 41
   4.1. Herbart-Zillerism as a pedagogical guideline 41
   4.2. The teacher training college of Tornio 45

5. The first steps toward professionalism 49

6. The development of the teacher personality 55
   6.1. Emphasis of academic subjects 55
   6.2. Playing the harmonium and singing 56
   6.3. Practical skills for life 58
   6.4. Gymnastics, games, and sports 61

7. Process factors that strengthen the teacher image 65
   7.1. Practical training at the Training school 65

   7.2. Supplementary activities and their impact to the teacher image 72
   7.3. Controlling students' free time 76

8. The formation of the teacher image 83
   8.1. The first steps toward professionalism 83
   8.2. The development of the teacher personality 84
   8.3. Process factors that strengthened the teacher image 85

9. Conclusion 87

Resources 91

1. Introduction

The basic factors of a Finnish teacher's professional identity are defined by society[1]. Teaching is bound by culture and is moulded both through the skills required for daily work and a society's expectations of the task of a teacher. As society changes, so does the role of a teacher.[2] A teacher's task is not only to impart the prevalent social and cultural values to his or her pupils, but also to act as a force for societal reform. A teacher should be a critic and a reformer, guiding pupils toward critical thinking concerning the prevalent conditions. Criticism and reflection make societal reform possible.[3]

Earlier research focusing on the Finnish teacher training system has focused mostly on the subjects taught at teacher training colleges[4]. Practical skills and other college activities, on the other hand, have received less attention. How should the teacher image be studied from an historical perspective? What factors influence the teacher image? In this study, the teacher image will be examined from the following perspectives: the first step toward the teaching profession; the development of the teacher personality; and the process factors that strengthen the teacher image. With the help of the source material, I will study the requirements of entrance tests for teacher training programmes, the selection of applicants, the teaching of practical skills, and what is emphasised in college supplementary activities.

The aim of this research is to clarify the teacher training process and to focus on the following perspectives: What kinds of abilities do practical

---

1   Värri 2001, 37.
2   Lauriala 2000, 89; Luukkainen 2005, 17–19;Värri 2002, 56.
3   Heikkinen 2001, 124.
4   Halila 1950, 78–79; Heikkinen 2003, 130–131; Hyyrö 2006, 5; Iisalo 1989, 236–237; Kuikka 1978, 104; Lahdes 1961, 7, 28–32; Nurmi 1989, 20; Paksuniemi 2009; Stormbom 1991, 119–121; Tamminen 1998, 19–20.

skills and supplementary activities provide for the formation of the teacher image and its development? The study also aims to clarify the Finnish teacher image and how teachers mature into the profession from an historical perspective. Teacher training provided at Finnish colleges is somewhat uniform. Textbooks, learning requirements, and the skill and knowledge required of students are mostly similar.[5] This study investigates the traditional teaching at teacher training colleges by closely examining the activities of the Teacher Training College of Tornio during the years of 1921–1945. It was a college for women.

---

5   Halila 1963; Heikkinen 1995; Isosaari 1961; Nurmi 1995; Paksuniemi 2009; Rinne 1989.

2. Theoretical starting points

2.1. The Finnish teacher image—requirements and changes

The actions and work of a teacher are shaped by curricula as well as various guidelines and desires as to the kind of behaviour that teachers are expected to emulate[6]. Curricula form a model for teachers to follow since social goals and influence are transferred into the curricula during the planning stage[7]. Before the development of curricula and the various processes of reform that have been undertaken, teaching was primarily a top-down, book-centred system. The textbook acted as a practical curriculum in the absence of any official material.[8] Behind the textbooks, on the other hand, is an operationalized curriculum that can be adjusted by the authorities. Textbooks are controlled either by the state or some other entity that decides on the approval or rejection of the material.[9] Due to reforms in 1985 and 1994, responsibility for teaching was transferred to the teachers and schools. The role of the teacher in the Finnish school society changed. The teacher became a supervisor, planned his or her own work, and was expected to work in cooperation with various parties, such as the students, parents, and other teachers. Today, teachers must work in an atmosphere of dynamic change, which increases pressure and expectations concerning teachers.[10]

A teacher's ability to influence his or her school's society is minimal until he or she establishes a sufficiently strong position within the working

---

6   Lapinoja 2006, 155.
7   Kujala 2008, 48–49.
8   Ropo & Huopainen 2001, 78, 86.
9   Kuikka 2001, 90–92.
10 Lauriala 2000, 89–90; Ropo & Huopainen 2001, 78, 86, 90; Syrjäläinen 1997; Syrjäläinen 2002; Syrjäläinen 2009, 145.

community. Until then, a new teacher adapts, with support if necessary, to the existing operating methods in the school. The turnover of personnel can be important for a school society's development and adaptation to new perspectives.[11] Certain professions favour certain personality types, which in turn, contain their own kind of structure of motive. Motivation can be distinguished according to whether it is based on individual values and preferences or on external factors. External motivational factors relate to professional role learning, which is a process of professional socialisation. Professional socialisation refers to the acceptance of values required for certain professions and the adaptation to the norms and rules of the professional environment. These internal factors and external forces can also work together, which strengthens motivation.[12]

According to researchers, *teacherhood* is connected to the teaching profession. When speaking of the teaching profession, the special professional skills, competencies, and education required by the profession are emphasised, and the profession is clearly distinct with its own collective identity.[13] In Finland, the teaching profession is also associated with ethicality, as the teacher makes choices in his or her work that are influenced by various values and norms[14]. The teacher's morality and ethical model are defined in the profession as a responsibility that is evident in a teacher's actions[15]. The teacher's professional and ethical challenges are in constant interaction with each other, and teachers cannot differentiate their professional role from its moral nature. Moral and professional thought go hand in hand, forming practical knowledge that a teacher needs in his or her work.[16]

Values are choices that are learnt from the environment, are permanent, and are target oriented. Education is usually considered to have been

---

11 Heikkinen 2001, 125.
12 Jussila & Lauriala 1989, 4–5, 69; Vonk & Schras 1987, 108. See Perho 1982, 19.
13 Lapinoja 2006, 144–146; Luukkainen 2000, 78; Rinne & Jauhiainen 1988, 59–61.
14 Atjonen 2005, 64–65; Luukkainen 2005, 41; Pursiainen 2002, 37; Syrjäläinen 2009, 145; Tirri 2002, 23–26.
15 Tirri 1996, 84–85.
16 Paksuniemi 2009; Tirri 1999a, 22–24. See Ahonen 2002, 66.

successful when the students have learnt the prevailing values and moral code in a society and behave within the boundaries set by these guidelines. Norms are conceptual rules that consist of commands and prohibitions, as well as permitted and recommended acts. Society sets expectations for the behaviour of individuals in accordance with the norms. The content of the norms and degree to which behaviour is required to conform may vary, but the norm is never far from actual action. As norms are based on values, different groups and communities, including professional groups, all have their own norms.[17]

In ethical education, emphasis is placed on the correct way of thinking, while in moral education, the focus is on the significance of the right action. Ethical education aims at the independent awareness of the sources of values.[18] Ethical education takes place in real situations, such as where moral norms have been broken. Ethical education is distinct from ethical teaching, which takes place on a symbolic level, such as in the teacher's speech, in academic subjects, and in textbooks.[19] The teacher's own ethical views act as the basis for the teacher's decisions[20]. Morals have always been historically and socially defined, and in casual discussion, they can be likened to good manners or respect for traditions[21]. Moral action is based on the prevailing rules in a society[22]. Moral education focuses on the significance of doing what is right and is usually associated with approved manners. Until the end of the 1900s, the term "decency" was often used to refer to ethics and morals.[23]

When examining the trends in the teaching profession from the end of the 19th century until the turn of the 21st century, change appears to have taken place regarding the special features of the teaching profession. In his book *Kasvatus- ja opetusoppi* (Pedagogy and Didactics), Wallin (1893) outlined the characteristics that were required of students

---

17 Allardt 1986, 51; Antikainen et al. 2000, 22–26.
18 Harris 1992, 2.
19 Paksuniemi 2009; Takala 1997, 47.
20 Tirri 1999b, 36.
21 Airaksinen 1988, 10; Sipilä 1998, 81; Uusikylä 2002, 10.
22 Lindqvist 2002, 76; Pietarinen & Poutanen 1998, 12.
23 Launonen 2000, 55–61, 155.

accepted into a teacher training college, including physical and mental health and an inner calling.[24] In the 19th century, there were clear ethical norms that were recorded in school laws. For example, teachers were required to relate positively to their country and to religion. The work of teachers was closely monitored, and if a teacher's behaviour deviated from those requirements, then he/she became the focus of general disapproval. These requirements were firmly enforced until the 1940s.[25] An individual who felt a calling to become a teacher was expected to concentrate on his or her work and to develop himself. Teacher was expected to sacrifice personal time for work and to consider tasks outside of the school day as part of his or her professional responsibilities.[26] Historically, the teaching profession in Finland has attracted individuals who felt that teaching was a calling or a mission and felt that they received "inner rewards" for their efforts[27].

In the past, a "calling" often referred to a task that an individual felt called to by God for which he must sacrifice both himself and his dreams by dedicating himself to his work. A teacher who has felt a calling sees his or her work as a service and feels that he or she has something to contribute to the field of education and to the lives of one's pupils. Teacher's actions often extend outside of the classroom. A calling includes a strong sense of morality with regard to one's work. Nowadays, when speaking of a calling, we commonly use the term "commitment."[28] Research has shown that diligence, integrity, and orderliness have also been emphasised in requirements set for teachers[29]. Strong mental health was an early requirement for teachers, but this was later changed to model behaviour, musicality, Christian decency, and patriotism at the start of the 20th century. However, the other requirements set for teachers in the 19th century were still very influential. When recruiting teachers, a farming and rural

---

24   Wallin 1893, 222–224.
25   Kuikka 1993, 104–106; Paksuniemi 2009.
26   Asp 1969, 67–69; Kuikka 1993, 104–106; Paksuniemi 2009.
27   Jussila & Lauriala 1989, 18.
28   Estola & Syrjälä 2002, 85, 91, 96.
29   Paksuniemi 2009; Rinne 1986a, 205.

background was favoured, because people from rural areas were seen as having similar backgrounds as their pupils.[30]

In the 1940s, teaching was still seen as a calling, but teachers were also required to have democratic values, a sense of direction and presentation skills, and to be decent and upstanding. The Christian and decency requirements were influential until the 1950s. Individuals from the middle and upper classes in urban areas became interested in the teaching profession and began to apply for teacher training.[31]

In the 1960s and 1970s, the teaching profession evolved to be seen as an academic profession, and the term "calling" was dropped in favour of "civil servant" ethics. A civil servant worked for the state or a municipality and strictly adhered to collective agreements and trade organisation guidelines.[32] Requirements for the teaching profession were presentation skills, the right attitude, and an interest in the job. Teachers were seen as technicians;[33] that is, someone who was able to utilise various observations and tools in his or her work. New teaching technical models allowed for a new kind of teaching. Kuikka (1993) drew a parallel between a teacher who has felt a calling and the concept of a conscientious conscious teacher. Such a teacher placed emphasis on his or her tasks because he or she saw himself as having an influence on society.[34] From the 1970s onwards, value was placed on a teacher's presentation skills, success in studies, suitability for the task, and general interest in the field[35].

Between 1950 and 1970, entrance examinations remained fairly similar with regard to structure and content. In 1971, however, a change occurred in the selection of applicants. Instead of simply being required to take an entrance examination that demonstrated knowledge, students also took a personality test. It was removed in 1975, however, and as such was

---

30 Hyry & Hyvönen 2003, 64–78; Paksuniemi 2009; Rinne 1989, 193–197; Rinne 1986a, Rinne & Jauhiainen 1988, 219–220;Värri 2001, 36–42.
31 Haavio 1969, 18–21, 69, 92–93; Paksuniemi 2009; Rinne 1986a, 111–122; Rinne 1989, 193–197; Rinne & Jauhiainen 1988, 223–225.
32 Asp 1969, 67–69; Kuikka 1993, 104–108.
33 Kuikka 1993, 108–110; Simola 1995, 233–251;Värri 2001, 39–40.
34 Kuikka 1993, 108–110.
35 Rinne 1989, 205.

not present in the entrance examination process for very long.[36] Another change was that a teaching practicum carried out in a real classroom was introduced in place of fictional teaching. This reform was retained until 1996, even though it began to fall out of favour. From 1988 to 1990 all Finnish teacher training units, with the exception of Joensuu, implemented the practicum as part of the entrance examinations, but it was eventually removed permanently in 1998. The suitability of an applicant to be a teacher was evaluated using a special presentation or analytical tasks and an interview.[37] The reason for adapting an authentic teaching practicum was research that had shown that the fictional teaching was a reliable tool for predicting future teaching skills. The practicum paid attention to the structuring and coherent processing of the subject being taught. Interaction with the students was also an aspect that was evaluated. In 1977, a change occurred in the selection of applicants for teacher training, as attention was no longer paid on an official level to the applicant's background, personality traits, or nature.[38]

In the 1980s, professional ethics became part of the requirements, and lifelong learning was emphasised, wherein teachers were seen as professionals who thought didactically, analysed teaching situations, and evaluated the influence of his or her actions on teaching. He or she was expected to seek continuous personal and professional development and to be flexible in his or her tasks. The civil servant was shifting from being an expert back to feeling a calling.[39] The external requirements for a model citizen, which were required for acceptance into a teacher training program in the 2000s, lost significance. For example, an earlier requirement of "flawless speech" was removed in 2007. Another change in the acceptance process that took place in the same year was a project, which replaced work and qualification points as pre-application criteria with a book exam.[40]

---

36 Rinne 1986a, 176–177.
37 Räihä 2010, 52, 116.
38 Rinne 1986a, 179.
39 Krokfors 1998, 78, 80–81; Kuikka 1993, 104–106; Leino & Leino 1989, 15–22; Rinne & Jauhiainen 1988, 234;Värri 2001, 40–42.
40 Räihä 2010, 50.

Regardless of the changes in requirements throughout the last few centuries, to this day, teachers are professionals who have undergone a thorough screening process. In its own way, the task of entrance examinations is to construct status for the teaching community: If it is difficult to enter the profession, then the status of those accepted into the profession remains higher than in such professions for which the application requirements are few. Entrance examinations, therefore, have a consolidative, cohesive, and strengthening effect on the profession. Such stringent entrance examinations are used to distinguish teaching from other professions.[41]

According to Lindén (2001), even though teachers' external exemplarity has been lost over the years, inner exemplarity has only changed its form[42]. Nevertheless, changes in society are reflected in the profession, and the work is not seen as a defining factor in a teacher's life. Over the decades, the earlier interest in a teacher's background and his or her reputation—demonstrated by the application selection process—has waned, and an interest in his or her ability to complete tasks has increased.[43]

2.2. Teacher training, professional development and maturity

Much research on the application process for teacher training colleges and the selection of applicants as first steps toward the teaching profession has been carried out over the decades,[44] but there has been far less historical research on the matter. The purpose of teacher training is to train students to become teachers. In Finland, the teachers at the teacher training colleges or universities select and teach new students for teacher training. This shows that those involved in the teaching profession operate in rather close

---

41 Kemppinen 2007, 190.
42 Lindén 2001, 18–27.
43 Rinne 1989, 206–207.
44 Jussila & Lauriala 1989; Perho 1982.

circles.[45] Current teachers select individuals with professional capabilities from groups of applicants[46].

The development of a teacher's personality during the teacher training is, however, a wider entity. Teacher training strives to consciously influence the growth of a student as a teacher, as well as his or her pedagogical thinking and ideology of control.[47] Teacher training aims to influence the student's thought and actions, which, in turn, assist the development of teacher professionalism[48]. The teacher has an important role in ensuring that the student feels a sense of belonging to and identifies with the profession. This furthers the formation of his or her professional identity. The development of a professional identity is a life-long process, during which an individual adopts information, skills, and values relating to the professional field as well as the external identifiers of the profession.[49] It is unlikely that any other profession has such long-term and thorough training as the teaching profession, as teacher training and socialisation into the teaching profession begins as early as the first years of comprehensive school. When entering teacher training, future teachers already have certain beliefs and impressions of teaching, learning, and school.[50]

Research on the professional development of teachers can be approached from different perspectives. A professional development model drawn up by Niemi (1989) includes three central focus areas: professional skills, personality, and the cognitive process. There is a lot of interaction between these focus areas. Interaction dominates between these three. Professional skill requirements relate to the planning and implementation of the teaching process, as well as the evaluative abilities required by teaching responsibilities. Personality factors include a healthy and strong self-image and the development of a personal teaching style. The cognitive process requires the teacher to have thorough understanding of information and the ability to impart the most important parts of this information

---

45   Luukkainen 2005, 41; Paksuniemi 2009.
46   Paksuniemi 2009.
47   Määttä 1989, 154.
48   Lauriala 1997, 75.
49   Mäntylä 2007, 92–94.
50   Lauriala 2000, 90. See Kelsall & Kelsall 1969, 14.

to students.[51] The professional development of a teacher can also be studied from the perspectives of personal development, professionalization, and socialisation[52].

Heikkinen (2002) states that a professional identity is constructed in teaching[53]. Together with Huttunen, he examines teaching from three perspectives: a personal perspective, a professional perspective, and personal identity. The personal perspective examines the requirements for a model teacher. From a professional perspective, the focus is on how a socially separate professional group is constructed by teachers. The personal perspective investigates finding oneself as a teacher. These three perspectives form the teacher's virtues, or characteristics that a teacher aims to achieve[54].

MacIntyre (1984) defines a virtue as follows:

"A virtue is an acquired human quality, the possession and exercise of which tends to enable us to achieve those goods which are internal to practices and the lack of which effectively prevents us from achieving any such goods"[55]. He names three historic virtue theories, of which the "homeric" perspective could be said to explain the action of a teacher according to virtues: "A virtue is a quality which enables an individual to discharge his or her social role."[56] The definition of a Finnish teacher's virtue has changed from the end of the 19th century to the turn of the 21st century, and it appears to be bound to prevailing values in society. In the 19th century, the virtues required of a teacher at a Finnish primary school were defined in detail, and prospective teachers were educated in these virtues during their studies at teacher training colleges.[57] Expectations for teacher virtues still exist, but they are not as extensive. Nowadays, more

---

51 Niemi 1989, 82–87.
52 Vonk & Schras 1987, 108.
53 Heikkinen 2002, 101.
54 Heikkinen & Huttunen 2007, 15–25.
55 MacIntyre 1984, 190.
56 Ibid., 189–191.
57 Hyyrö 2006; Nurmi 1965; Nurmi 1996; Paksuniemi 2009; Rantala 2005; Rinne 1986a; Rinne 1986b.

deviations are permitted.[58] The areas on which teacher training has historically placed emphasis are products of their own time, but nevertheless their influence is still felt today. In current teacher training, there is special emphasis on the development of a teacher's pedagogical studies,[59] a strong connection between theoretical training and practice,[60] and wide-ranging teacherhood that is influenced by different factors.[61]

According to Pickle (1985), maturity in the teaching profession is the result of a long-term process. She described three dimensions of this process: the professional dimension, the personal dimension, and the process dimension. The professional dimension is the individual's adaptation to the teaching professional group or the profession. As the teacher matures, she or he moves on from the practical, applicable use of information to become a user of more theoretical and academic information. The professional dimension can be evaluated by following the increase in the teacher's amount of esoteric information. This refers to an increase in the teacher's amount of profession-related knowledge. The accumulation of esoteric information begins with practical information and develops into the ability to adopt theories and academic research.[62]

The development of a willingness and readiness to serve is another way in which the professional dimension can develop. Here, the teacher works more for the benefit of society rather than for his or her own benefit. This is related to awareness of a calling. The third form of the professional dimension is affective neutrality. This means that the teacher carries out his or her work while in control of his or her feelings and treats his or her pupils equally and objectively.[63] According to Pickle, the personal dimension is realised when the teacher is conscious of himself or herself and his or her pupils. The more aware a teacher is of himself and his or her own life, the better the teacher is able to understand his or her pupils and their different

---

58 Heikkinen & Huttunen 2007, 25.
59 OPM 2001, 13–16.
60 Kosunen & Mikkola 2001.
61 E.g., Jussila 2009, 66–69; Lauriala 2000; Niemi 1992; Niemi 1995; Niemi 1998; Niemi & Tirri 1997; Syrjäläinen 1995.
62 Pickle 1985, 55–58.
63 Ibid., 55–56.

backgrounds. The personal dimension also includes the ambition to develop oneself as a teacher. This means, for example, following literature in the field and participating in supplementary training. The development of a personal style is the third component in the personal dimension. It refers to the development of the teacher into a teaching personality through his or her own choices and trial and error.[64]

The process dimension refers to the teacher's thought development and actions in his or her work. Teaching requires the skill of thinking flexibly, broadly, and rationally, as situations in the classroom change unexpectedly several times a day. Rational thinking relates to the development of critical thinking. In practice, this means that the teacher is able to make decisions in his or her work and is able to explain and, if necessary, defend his or her decisions. The third skill included in the process dimension is perspectivity. A teacher should be able to examine his or her ideas and problems from a wide perspective. This, in turn, helps decision-making.[65]

Pickle sets no time limits for professional maturity, as even a large number of years spent in the field do not automatically guarantee professional maturity. Pickle says that certain dimensions are achieved in teaching, whereas socialisation can be influenced early in the teacher training process. She states:

"Some of the dimensions may best be taught and learned through a developmental growth paradigm, whereas other qualities might best be socialized or resocialized early in the teacher's education and then maintained."[66]

Pickle's comprehensive theory on the professional maturity of teachers gives rise to the question: "How does teacher training influence the creation of a foundation necessary for the achievement of these three dimensions?" What is the process that a prospective teacher undergoes before it is possible to achieve the dimensions set out by Pickle? The contemplation triggered by Pickle's theory has influenced the format of this study. Perspectives that are significant to this study must be examined before

---

64 Ibid., 56–57.
65 Ibid., 57–58.
66 Ibid., 58.

moving on to the application of Pickle's theory. In this study, teacherhood is seen as a theoretical phenomenon that is influenced by societal reality, curriculum, and the school society (see Figure 1).

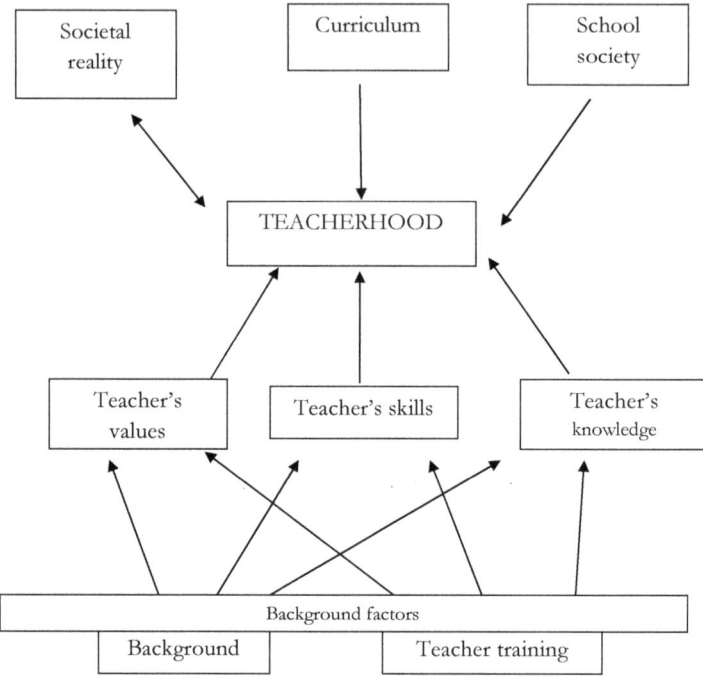

Figure 1. Teacherhood depicted as a theoretical phenomenon.

The teacher role is also influenced by a teacher's personal values, skills, and knowledge as well as their teacher training, background factors (such as experiences at home and in school), and personal characteristics.

2.3. The teacher image

In this study, the formation of a Finnish teacher image at teacher training colleges is seen as a subconcept of the teacherhood concept, as shown in Figure 2.

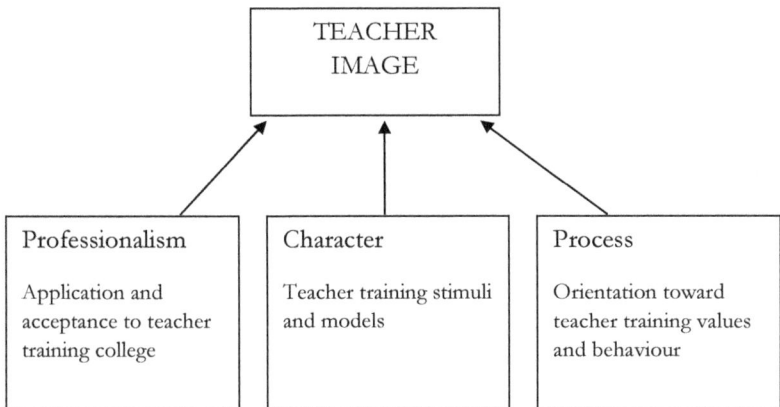

Figure 2. The formation of the teacher image in teacher training.

The *teacher image* is an image developed by the teacher himself during the teacher training process of his own role as a teacher. The prospective teacher's growth toward professional maturity begins as he or she applies for training as the application for teacher training pushes the student toward the start of professionalism. Teacher training learning materials act to adapt his or her personality, while shaping the teacher image, and supplementary activities during teacher training act as a process factor that strengthens the teacher image.

Research questions

The task of this study is to examine the historical background behind the Finnish teacher image from 1921 to 1945. The matter will be examined using information from applicant selection, textbooks used in teacher training, and other activities.

The following questions were set for this study:

(1.) Professionalism: What kind of students applied for and were accepted into teacher training colleges?

The answer to this question will be investigated by researching the kind of individuals who desired to become teachers and the kind of individuals who applied for teacher training. In order to investigate this question, the study will examine the requirements set by teacher training entrance examinations and the capabilities of accepted students on probation.

(2.) Personality: What personality traits did the learning materials emphasized in teacher training colleges?

The textbooks and materials used in the teacher training colleges were important tools for how the college students' teacher image was influenced and how their practical skills were developed. The content of the textbooks and learning materials will be examined (with regard to practical skills), as well as written material relating to teaching practices.

(3.) Process: What kinds of skills, values, and behaviour were encouraged at teacher training colleges?

This study aims to examine the kind of teacher image outlined in supplementary activities at teacher training colleges. This study will search for the types of process factors that were used to strengthen the teacher image. The study will focus on the years between 1921 and 1945. The start of the period to be examined falls at a time when the wider formation of teacher training was taking place and the training was further clarified. The year 1945 was chosen as an upper limit because teacher training in Finland began to be standardised at this point and only partially changed after that time. The aim of the study is to examine the foundation of Finnish teacher training, its roots, and how the students' teacher image was formed during the teacher training process.

2.4. Method of research and source material

This study concerns the history of education and utilises primary sources to search for answers to the research questions that are posed. Research into the history of education should first and foremost be based on primary sources, which should be as diverse as possible and are often found in archives. The researcher should have access to information that is as close as possible to the issue at hand or to the original source of the information.[67]

---

67   Paksuniemi 2009; Renvall 1965, 199, 203–204.

This method of thinking emphasises the value of the original source. However, one should also consider the kind of questions to which answers are being sought using these sources.[68] The investigation of this topic requires that teacher training college activities be considered as part of the history of education in Finland. The aims, methods, and terms of the education are bound to cultural, social, and historical conditions.[69]

The teacher training college institution is one system component of Finnish society, and its functional task has traditionally been to produce teachers. The central aim of this study is to compile various factors into one historical unit that will explain the basis of Finnish teacher training. The study concentrates on the activities of one Finnish teacher training college in detail—the Teacher Training College of Tornio—and only analyses the female students at this institution. The focus of the analysis is on structural analysis, which is when a researcher seeks to describe how a certain phenomenon occurred during a given time in a given environment.

The source material for this study includes archival sources, textbooks were used at the teacher training college, and academic year reports, *Annuals*. Pedagogical texts, such as teaching guides and curricula, reveal the aims and models for teaching and education. They act as ideological tools because the textbooks demonstrate what was considered important to teach during the period in question. The analysis focuses on the features that were highlighted in the textbooks. The views they contain do not reveal the entire truth concerning the overall image of teacher training; however, they do provide their own perspective for the period in question.

---

68 Kalela 2000, 89, 92–93, 97.
69 Antikainen et al. 2000, 12.

3. At the roots of the Finnish school system

3.1. Aiming to produce educated citizens for society

In 1723, a royal decree stated that parents had to teach their children to read or send them to be taught by the parish under threat of a fine. In 1773, confirmation classes were made compulsory, and in 1776, it was declared that the literacy skills of parishioners had to be checked before they took their first Holy Communion. The education organised by the church emphasised teaching literacy and learning the catechism and Christian doctrines. Supporters of the primary school ideology advocated separating education from the administration of the church and making it the responsibility of society, but the church did not approve, fearing that the teaching at primary schools would be too liberal. The content of the Finnish school system and the direction of education were defined by the church until the middle of the 19th century. Beginning in the Reformation, the cornerstones of education had been the Lord's Prayer, the Confession of Faith, and the Ten Commandments.[70]

Uno Cygnaeus (1810–1888), who founded the Finnish primary school system, adopted the basic idea of Pestalozzi's pedagogy,[71] which states that investing in the education of individuals is important from a social development perspective. Each adult was to make sure that children experienced "even development of body and soul." Schools were to teach both theoretical and practical subjects, such as crafts and gymnastics. The task of the school was to make sure that information became internalised in the student.[72] Cygnaeus thought that the primary school system should be founded on a Christian basis but should also teach practical skills. He felt

---

70 Lipponen 2003.
71 Iisalo 1989, 122–123.
72 Cygnaeus 1910; Iisalo 1989, 122–123; Tuomaala 2004.

that the primary school should not be simply a place to read and recite and that it should provide a basic education for the entire population. Cygnaeus strove to invoke love toward the underprivileged. His aim was to develop the primary school based on crafts, as education was to encourage the development of pupils' visual, observational, and aesthetic understanding and to teach them how to use tools.[73]

Cygnaeus' thoughts clashed completely with those of Johan V. Snellman, (1806–1881) who believed that the primary school system's most important task was "cognitive education"[74]. Snellman's views were largely based on Hegel's thoughts, and he often turned to this philosophy, which supported abstract thinking and reasoning. Snellman felt that the school system had succeeded in its task if a pupil fell in love with learning.[75] The most fundamental difference between Cygnaeus' and Snellman's opinions was that Snellman considered the school system's principal task as imparting cognitive education, while Cygnaeus felt that pupils should develop in a balanced manner. Snellman's thoughts prevailed, as the primary school developed into a system that emphasised knowledge. According to Snellman, the path from nature to culture, from necessity to freedom, and from senselessness to sense was accompanied by discipline and varied depending on the pupil's age. He felt that there were three places of education: the home, the nation state, and society. He demanded strict school discipline, stating:

"We consider discipline to give the most support to education." Snellman emphasised that the task of the school system was to produce socially productive citizens, members of society who followed the law and displayed good behaviour. Pupils were indirectly taught the importance of abiding by the law through the implementation of order and discipline at school. The primary task of a school was seen as imparting education on the entire population.[76]

The starting point for mass education was giving individuals a life goal of developing society. The virtue of an individual was seen as representing

---

73 Cygnaeus 1903, 124; Isosaari 1961; Tuomaala 2004.
74 Iisalo 1989, 123–124.
75 Koski 1999, 24; Lehmusto 1951, 231–233.
76 Melin 1980; Ojakangas 2003; Paksuniemi 2009.

the virtue of society as a whole. Each person was to see himself as both a unique individual, responsible morally and spiritually, and part of something larger—a common good—both secular and spiritual. As Hegel's school of thought merged with the traditional Lutheran morals prevalent in Finland, the model of good children and educated citizens was based on the idea of dialogue between the decent individual, the God-fearing individual, and the development of a productive citizen. Behind the idea of educating citizens in a patriotic and virtuous manner was the aim of unifying the people and raising the general level of education in order to avoid having to go experience any further conflict similar to that experienced during the Finnish Civil War. Socio-moral aims, on the other hand, were based on the traditional Lutheran methods of education.[77] In this model, it was believed that children are a gift from God, meant not for parents, but for heaven. Lutheranism's focus on daily devotion and living dutifully emphasised the significance of children's education and the divine origin of civil virtues.[78] Snellman and Cygnaeus disagreed, particularly on the issue of primary education. Snellman wanted primary education to be the task of the family, while Cygnaeus felt that young children should be included in the school system. In other words, this was a question of the relationship between education at home and the primary school system.[79]

3.2. Christianity and decency through discipline and order

The Decree on Primary Education (Kansakouluasetus), came into effect in 1866. As a result of the act, teaching in Finland began to take on uniform and ordered features.[80] The act stipulated that pupils should attend primary

---

77 Koski 1999.
78 Kuikka 2003.
79 Lipponen 2003.
80 Decree on Primary Education [Kansakouluasetus] 1866. See Paksuniemi 2009; Valta 2002.

school for 6 years in urban areas and 4 years in rural areas[81]. In towns and cities, the age limit for pupils was 8 to 14 years. The decree also specified the maximum number of pupils in a class: there were to be no more than 40 pupils in the first grade and a maximum of 60 pupils in other grades.[82] The purpose of the act was not to make the primary school a school for everybody, but instead to push it in a certain direction[83]. Primary schools were to be founded in towns and cities so that all willing 8- to 12-year olds could attend. Primary schools were divided into lower and upper primary schools. In the lower primary schools, girls and boys were taught in the same classes, but in the upper primary schools, they were taught separately.[84] On June 27, 1889, this law changed, and in existing primary schools, girls and boys could be taught together if conditions so required[85]. The Decree on Primary Education did not specify that education was compulsory, and it did not obligate municipalities and towns or cities to establish primary schools[86].

The sociopolitical background of these schools was visible in the primary school teaching programme. The aim of the schools was to teach children diligence and to diversify their livelihood by teaching crafts, for example. Finland was a global pioneer in the teaching of crafts. It was important to learn how to manufacture day-to-day utensils and to learn skills for daily life; the aim was for students to return to agricultural work after completing their education.[87] Pupils were a part of the family labour in agricultural communities, and agricultural work dictated a child's participation in education. As such, children's attendance at school was irregular.[88]

Christianity was clearly visible in the curricula, and the teacher's task was to instil a fear of God into the children, along with gratitude and trust

---

81   Nurmi 1981, 39.
82   Decree on Primary Education [Kansakouluasetus] 1866.
83   Halila 1949a, 368–369.
84   Decree on Primary Education [Kansakouluasetus] 1866.
85   Merciful Decree of Imperial Majesty [Keisarillisen Majesteetin Armollinen Asetus] 1889.
86   Decree on Primary Education [Kansakouluasetus] 1866.
87   Halila 1949b, 184–285.
88   Lipponen 2003.

in God, and to encourage the pupils to display this fear of God in all situations through obedience toward their parents and teachers.[89] The Christian decency educational morals favoured features such as a pure heart, teetotalism, humility, obedience, a sense of duty, charity, helpfulness, diligence, gratitude, decency, honesty, and chivalry. If children were good, a relationship could be formed between the child and God. On the other hand, a bad child bullied and ridiculed others, lied, stole, was disobedient, and was careless and lazy.[90]

The Decree on Primary Education included methods of punishment that teachers could use if a pupil did not abide by the school rules. These did not just apply to disobedient pupils, but also to those who were lazy and careless. Before punishing a pupil, the teacher had to give a warning.[91] If necessary, the teacher was permitted to use the following forms of punishment: make the pupil sit further down (pupils sat in order in class, and the lazy and careless student moved seats); separate the pupil from other pupils; scold and warn the child in front of the class; place the pupil in detention; use physical discipline, which meant spanking the pupil's palm six times with a cane in front of the class; and, as a last resort, exclusion from the school.[92]

The Decree on Primary Education gave detailed instructions on who could give punishment and how the instructions should be used and interpreted. Scolding, for example, was an immediate reaction by the teacher to a pupil's disobedience, and separation from other pupils usually meant being sent to a corner. The severity of the punishment depended on the seriousness of the pupil's behaviour, such as rebellious behaviour or questioning the teacher's authority.[93] Other methods of discipline used included hair pulling, hitting with a pointer stick, and standing behind the blackboard[94]. The decree created a foundation based on which changes to punishments were made later on. The regulations set out by the decree were

---

89   Cygnaeus 1910, 269; Haavio 1941, 49; Salo 1934, 12–13.
90   Koski 1999.
91   Valta 2002.
92   Decree on Primary Education [Kansakouluasetus] 1866.
93   Heporauta 1945, 83; Valta 2002.
94   Valta 2002.

applied to primary schools throughout Finland with very few changes mostly related to the use of names used for punishments. The methods of discipline set out in the Decree on Primary Education did not change significantly in later acts and decrees. The most significant change took place as a decrease in the number of methods of discipline, such as the prohibition of physical discipline in 1914.[95]

Pupils were to be educated with a fear of God, a sense of patriotism, respect for the law and authorities, good manners, and diligence, and as such, discipline was strict. Military discipline was upheld during lessons; for example, there were detailed instructions on how to put your hand up during class.[96] Primary school guidelines emphasised strict and detailed order. The novelty of the primary school system and the large numbers of pupils in classes also contributed to the need for strict and orderly discipline. Some pupils adapted well to this strict discipline, but it caused reluctance to attend school in others. Restless students found it difficult to sit still, as they were not used to doing so. The number of punishments during the early years of the primary school system was influenced by the fact that the pupils were unfamiliar with the practices at the schools. Many pupils' parents had not attended school and were unable to help their children with the matter. Nor did the parents value school attendance, which was visible in the children's' weak motivation to study.

Disturbances were a problem in the early years of the Finnish primary school system, but discipline was not seen as a problem once the pupils had become used to the customs of the school. On the other hand, there were also children who were "subservient" toward the school, and there was no great need to punish such pupils. In addition, the voluntary nature of the primary school facilitated the situation, as badly behaved children took themselves out of school.[97]

One of the most important reforms at the end of the 19th century was the Decree on School Districts (Piirijakoasetus) issued on May 24, 1898; it promoted the establishment of upper primary schools in rural areas. The

---

95 Law on Physical Punishments [Laki ruumiillisista rangaistuksista] 1914.
96 Cygnaeus 1910, 52.
97 Valta 2002.

act stated that municipalities should establish schools despite the fact that, as yet, there was no compulsory education.[98] The Decree on School Districts was considered the first compulsory education law in Finland, even though it did not stipulate compulsory education. In accordance with the decree, rural municipalities were to form primary school districts and to ensure that each child of schooling age received teaching in his or her own mother tongue. A school had to be established if there were at least 30 willing children of schooling age in the school district. The journey to school could be no more than 5 kilometres.[99] This requirement could not be met in all areas, as many sparsely populated areas remained outside of the 5-kilometres restriction[100]. If more than 50 pupils attended the school, a new school had to be established or an assistant teacher had to be employed[101]. The decree was considered a breakthrough. The existing primary schools developed even further. In the first year following the decree, the number of pupils increased by around 5,000 pupils. There began to be more and more pupils in rural areas: just after the Decree on School Districts was passed, there were around 68,000 pupils, but in 1920, over 190,000 students were enrolled. The Decree on School Districts removed flaws in the primary school system even though primary education remained fairly deficient and scattered; as a result, the Finnish primary school system grew rapidly.[102]

3.3. The development of compulsory education

A law on compulsory education was proposed as early as 1910 but met with opposition from Tsar Nicholas II. The situation changed when Finland became independent in 1917 and a political decision could be made on

---

98 Decree on School Districts [Piirijakoasetus] 1898. See Paksuniemi 2009.
99 Decree on School Districts [Piirijakoasetus] 1898. See Nurmi 1983, 77.
100 Decree on School Districts [Piirijakoasetus] 1898.
101 Decree on School Districts [Piirijakoasetus]1898. See Heporauta 1945, 183.
102 Decree on Primary Education [Kansakouluasetus]1866. See Paksuniemi 2009; Tuunainen & Nevala 1986, 23.

the matter.[103] Compulsory education was opposed because it went against the general sense of justice, and that it would provoke discontent. These opinions were believed to weaken the status and respect for the primary school.[104] Parents also opposed the Act on Compulsory Education more strongly than first thought. One reason for this was ignorance, while another was their fear that respect for them as educators would weaken. This was largely a question of authority. Some of the parents considered primary school to be a factory with no sense of individuality. The primary education of children in rural areas was traditionally given at home and by the church. Until the 1840s, vergers were responsible for teaching, although only a few were able to teach arithmetic and writing. Even after the changes made to the Decree on Primary Education (Kansakouluasetus), people who had not received any education were able to provide a primary education to pupils, and, as a result, teachers were a diverse bunch.[105]

The main responsibility for teaching and education was still at home, but if parents were unable to ensure that children were satisfactorily taught reading, comprehension of their mother tongue, and Christian doctrine, then the church became responsible for their children's education, which they accomplished through touring schools that also taught writing, singing, and arithmetic.[106]

Even after the Decree on Primary Education was amended, primary education was slow to change. In practice, this meant that primary education was still mainly given at home under the supervision of priests, and the level of teaching varied greatly. This led to discussions on standardising primary education and the training of teachers.[107]

As temporary order regulations came into effect in 1918, it was recognised that Finland had to establish a sufficient number of 2-year training colleges for lower primary school teachers. This was the first step toward the development of Finnish lower primary education and the organisa-

---

103 Männistö 1994, 99.
104 Halila 1949b, 31–32.
105 Halila 1949a; Iisalo 1989, 16–17.
106 Decree on Primary Education [Kansakouluasetus] 1866. See Hyyrö 2006; Iisalo 1989.
107 Hyyrö 2006; Paksuniemi 2009.

tion of the necessary teacher training. Early years education merged with primary schools, and these became known as lower primary schools that were comprised of Grades 1 to 2 and taught children ages 7 to 8.[108]

The most visible change in the history of the school system took place around the time that Finland gained independence in the early 20th century. For the first time, Finns could establish a school based on the concept of an independent nation state. The school was seen as the most central influence in the process of constructing society. One developmental goal for the school system was the education and, simultaneously, the unification of the population. Mass education was seen as an important issue, as around 40% of children remained outside of regular teaching because of its voluntary nature.[109] Almost all children in urban areas in Finland and 68% of rural children attended primary school for at least a few years at the start of the 1920s[110]. At this time, the independence gained by Finland was still perceived as under threat, however. The nationalist ideology demanded control and discipline.[111]

After a wide discussion, compulsory education came into effect on April 15, 1921. According to the Act on Compulsory Education (Oppivelvollisuuslaki) it was mandated that all Finnish children attend school.[112] The Act on Compulsory Education of 1921 applied to children aged 7 to 12 and increased the amount of primary schools in rural areas. At the same time, the area in which primary schools were located expanded.[113] The implementation of compulsory education did not cause great change in cities and the wealthier parts of rural areas. The Act on Compulsory Education was a practice and form of national protection, which applied equally to rural and urban children. The responsibility of parents to care for and educate their children moved to the state, regardless of which societal group they belonged to. This was typical for the use of power in

---

108 Hyyrö 2006; Melin 1980; Paksuniemi 2009.
109 Kuikka 1991, 86–87.
110 Ahonen 2003, 68; Halila 1950, 13, 30.
111 Alapuro 1994, 299–303.
112 Act on Compulsory Education [Oppivelvollisuuslaki] 1921.
113 Act on Compulsory Education [Oppivelvollisuuslaki] 1921. See Heikkinen 2003, 135.

modern societies.[114] The act also included regulations for the 2-year primary schools[115].

The act did not, however, grant all schoolchildren equal status. Conditions in schools in rural areas and urban areas differed significantly. In urban areas, school attendance was so common that the Act on Compulsory Education was considered a formality. In addition, economical factors, especially during the Great Depression in the 1930s, hindered the establishment of new schools. Compulsory education was only fully implemented after the Second World War.[116]

Compulsory education was also used to help monitor citizens. Methods for this were, for example, obligation to attend school, literacy requirements, teacher training and supervision, consolidation of teaching in rural and outlying areas, and school networks created in urban areas. In several other European countries, too, school systems were subordinate to strong control,[117] although in Germany, the process was slowed by exceptional conditions in the countryside. Thanks to Cygnaeus, Finland caught up fairly quickly with other European countries concerning education. In the Netherlands, for example, primary school legislation had been in place since 1801, and legislation on primary schools came into effect in several Scandinavian countries at the start of the 19th century.[118] The situation in the United States was the same: There were many small schools and their activities were difficult to monitor, so regional differences remained for a long time.[119]

A three-level administrative model was constructed for the Finnish primary school system and was based on the principle of municipal self-administration. The highest level was a national authority, the National Board of General Education. The middle-level authorities were primary school inspectors. The lowest level consisted of regulations, acts, and de-

---

114 Tuomaala 2004, 75.
115 Nurmi 1981, 14–15; Rinne 1973, 97.
116 Act on Compulsory Education [Oppivelvollisuuslaki] 1921. See Hyyrö 2006; Paksuniemi 2009.
117 Green 1992, 1–2, 7, 11, 17–18, 62, 81.
118 Heikkinen 1995, 388; Heikkinen 2003, 135.
119 Petterson 1992, 73–74.

crees issued by the central government and which formed terms of reference for the activities of primary schools.[120] Compulsory education is considered to have unified the population as it meant that all children had to go to school. It was not, however, solely down to the Act on Compulsory Education that supporters of the "Reds" in the Finnish Civil War sent their children to the same school attended by their former adversaries, the Whites. The National Board of General Education consciously aimed to make the primary schools as nonpartisan as possible—a school for everyone. In trying to prevent the school system from forming a socially divisive institution, the National Board of General Education directed the schools' board of directors and the teachers' activities.[121]

Distrust toward the primary school system arose in working class circles, as the majority of primary school teachers had sided with the Whites during the Finnish Civil War. As a result, the number of children attending primary school decreased, although there were other factors that also contributed to the decrease.[122] In addition, the Senate and National Board of General Education monitored textbooks in Finnish primary and other schools. The state extended its authority into the classroom through curricula without having to be present during the actual teaching.[123]

Cygnaeus' idea that mothers who had attended primary school would give their children satisfactory primary education was partially realised up until the municipal primary school system became functional[124]. The implementation of compulsory education was connected to how active municipal authorities were. Only some municipalities carried out reforms in line with legislation: others took advantage of the regulations for the transitional period, according to which a school could be founded in rural areas within 16 months after the law came into effect, and it was possible to apply for a postponement to establish a school for a further period of 5 years. In urban areas, the law had to be obeyed within this time.[125]

---

120 Nurmi 1988, 147, 157, 177; Nurmi 1989, 22; Virta 2001, 49.
121 Rantala 2002, 174.
122 Rinne 1973, 95.
123 Lehtonen 1983, 15–20.
124 Iisalo 1989, 181–183; Nurmi 1989, 9–10.
125 Kuikka 1991, 87; Melin 1980, 282.

Differences in status were not only visible between the rural and urban areas. The Act on Compulsory Education did not remove all the problems that occurred in schools, but instead added to them, as compulsory education was applied to children of a certain age. The disciplinary measures permitted at primary schools were considered ineffective as the right to use physical discipline was removed from teachers and the exclusion of pupils from the school was no longer permitted after the Act on Compulsory Education came into effect. The removal of physical discipline was considered problematic as it was not possible to replace it with any other form of punishment. Its removal caused conflicting thoughts, as some people believed that the number of disciplinary measures permitted by the Decree on Primary Education were already few and far between. Furthermore, the prohibition of physical discipline was implemented at a bad time, as the spirit of the time was more restless than it had been in previous years. In order to ensure undisturbed studying, some wanted to retain physical discipline for exceptional cases, as primary schools would be otherwise powerless against ill-mannered pupils. The school system proposed the reinstatement of physical discipline, but the National Board of Education did not approve the proposal, saying that teachers should discuss discipline at home with the pupil's parents.[126] According to the Act on Compulsory Education, teachers had the right to punish pupils who did not follow the instructions and regulations of the school. The same applied to lazy or careless students who, despite warnings, did nothing to change their behaviour.[127]

Due to the novelty of the primary school system, there was no clear didactic policy during the early years of primary education. At the start of the 20th century, teaching became more uniform as a result of Herbartianism and reform pedagogy. Herbartianism emphasised teacher-led teaching of knowledge, while reform pedagogy concentrated on the pupil's freedom, the teacher as a supervisor, and on the work school ideology. The thought of practical learning began with social change and its needs. On the other hand, teacher-led teaching made pupils passive and caused rest-

---

126 Salmela 1935, 89–90.
127 Act on Compulsory Education [Oppivelvollisuuslaki] 1921.

lessness and difficulties with concentration. Teachers in Finnish primary schools worked largely within the methods of discipline permitted by the Decree on Primary Education, which was supplemented with additional guidelines to most likely prevent the misuse of punishment. No one was forced to use it, but it was feared that its permission would stigmatise all teachers. Lessons had to be made so interesting that none of the pupils would cause a disturbance.[128] The resulting meticulously planned lessons did not allow for the pupil's to move, express themselves, or gesture to each other, let alone socialise freely with their classmates[129].

The war years (1939 to 1945) significantly slowed the internal development of the Finnish school system. Connections with other countries broke down, and the Finnish national education ideal emerged. Models from other countries remained in the background. Discipline and order, as well as social education, were favoured in school life. Defence, voluntary, and club activities brought school and practical life closer together, and teachers increasingly became supervisors of extracurricular activities. The dispute between the Old and New School approaches was no longer spoken of, even though reform was on the horizon for theoretical pedagogy.[130]

Developments regarding the structure of primary school were taking place in other countries. In Denmark, the Netherlands, and Norway, pupils attended school for 7 years; in Russia, the mandated 7 years was changed to ten. In Switzerland, France, Germany, and Austria, students were required to attend school for 8 years; in Great Britain, the requirement was 9 years, including primary school; and in the United States, students attended school for 9 or 10 years. Basic education in Austria, Germany, and Finland lasted for 4 years.[131] In Sweden, compulsory primary education came into effect in 1936. There, primary school lasted 7 years and, in a few municipalities, an eighth school year was added. Sweden did not consider moving to a uniform school system until 1948. Their aim was to combine the 7-year primary school and the associated voluntary school into a single

---

128 Syväoja 2004; Valta 2002.
129 Syväoja 2004, 129.
130 Lahdes 1961, 153, 162–163.
131 Salo 1944, 371–372.

9-year comprehensive school. The change was justified with an increase in popular education and in making education more equal. In Denmark, a Decree on Primary Education was issued in 1937. There, students were required to attend school for 7 years.[132] In Finland, there was also discussion of changing the school system with regard to reforming the teacher training colleges, but these changes were not carried out until after the war.

---

132 Cavonius 1957, 22, 29.

4. Teacher training colleges in Finland

4.1. Herbart-Zillerism as a pedagogical guideline

The Herbart-Zillerist pedagogical approach, which had spread from Europe to Finland, influenced the education at the teacher training colleges. In Herbartianism, teaching was defined as an activity for both educating a person and encouraging them toward decency and inspiring an enthusiasm to try new things and gain more knowledge.[133] As early as the 1890s, lecturers in pedagogy at Finnish colleges had begun to apply the Herbart-Ziller pedagogical approach and its methods[134].

Johann Friedrich Herbart (1776–1841) was a German philosopher, psychologist, and founder of pedagogy as an academic discipline[135]. In the early 19th century, he created a philosophical and pedagogical system that saw success in Germany beginning in the 1860s, thanks to Tuiskon Ziller (1817–1882). Ziller was a German scientist who further developed the educational method created by Herbart.[136] As a result, this philosophy is known as Herbart-Zillerism. According to this method, the purpose of school was the development of a strong religious and decent nature in all students. Teachers were encouraged to utilise a diverse range of activities. Teaching was based on a teacher-led approach, whereby the teacher was responsible for deciding what was taught in the classroom. As such, the teacher held an important role in the classroom. Religion, literature, and history were all seen as important. They created a cultural-historic foundation upon which teaching was gradually built.[137] In the 1890s, the

---

133 Iisalo 1989, 152, 159–161.
134 Isosaari 1961, 150–152. See Lahdes 1961, 27.
135 Herbart 1806. See Hilgenheger 1993.
136 Ziller 1857; Ziller 1876.
137 Heikkinen 2003, 130–131; Iisalo 1989, 236–237; Lahdes 1961, 7, 28–32; Stormbom 1991, 119–121; Tamminen 1998, 19–20.

Herbart-Zillerism method began to affect the Finnish school system; for example, the curriculum used in the Finnish primary schools was based on this pedagogy. The curriculum encouraged students to have enthusiasm towards knowledge and to develop a strong, decent character. In addition, a common goal was to arouse regionalism, which invokes the love of one's country.[138]

Mikael Soininen became interested in Herbartianism in the 1890s. He worked as the leader of the teacher training college of Heinola and journeyed to Germany to visit the great Herbartian, Wilhelm Rein (1847–1929), which ignited the export of didactics to Finland. Soininen independently and brilliantly adapted the method for the Finnish school system.[139] He gained the reputation of being a Finnish champion of Herbartianism. In following Herbart's basic idea, Soininen believed that teaching should be educational and that it should pay special attention to decency.[140] One of Soininen's text books, General Pedagogy [Yleinen kasvatusoppi] starts with words:"Already for years, I have had in mind a desire to present for the Finnish researchers the main ideas of that educational trend that is named after Herbart and Ziller"[141]. According to Soininen, the goal of education was transmitting the moral-religious rearing into the bred by a strong authority[142]. Herbart-Zillerism was influencing the didactics books used in the teacher training colleges in Finland. Pedagogical text books, mainly written by Bruno Boxtröm, Aukusti Salo, the leader of the teacher training college of Heinola and Mikael Soininen, were used in the teacher training colleges. The text books emphasized regionalism, patriotism, decency and Christianity.[143]

At the start of the 20th century, Herbartianism had the greatest influence on the Finnish primary school system. It was seen as a clear solution to the discordant didactics of the late 19th century.[144] Herbartianism em-

---

138 Launonen 2000; Melin 1980.
139 Iisalo 1989, 236–237.
140 Iisalo 1989, 161–162.
141 Soininen 1923, 3.
142 E.g., Soininen 1911; Soininen 1923.
143 E.g., Boxtröm 1900; Salo 1926; Salo 1929; Soininen 1911; Soininen 1923.
144 Lahdes 1961, 87; Paksuniemi 2009.

phasised decency, enthusiasm toward trying new things, and concentration. Its ideology was based on a teacher-led approach, whereby the teacher was responsible for deciding what was taught in the classroom[145]. As such, the teacher had a central role in the classroom, and this was further underlined by the teacher's place on a podium[146]. The activity of the teacher, whereby the pupil was a passive recipient of information, was considered a weak point in Herbartianism[147]. The Herbart-Ziller teaching method began to spread and gain strength in Finland, even though it was falling out of favour in Central Europe at the same time[148].

In the world of pedagogy in the 1920s, there was talk of a new educational approach, which in practice meant mostly pupil-oriented working methods[149]. This approach was based on the concept of reform pedagogy, whose representatives opposed Herbart-Zillerism. They believed that learning had to include a certain kind of freedom and that pupil individuality had to be taken into account. The teacher was to take on the role of a supervisor. The representatives of reform pedagogy were of the opinion that Herbart-Zillerism concentrated too much on the development of intellect and favoured passive working methods. This caused unfavourable relationships between the pupil and teacher and between the pupil and classroom society. The New School criticised the Herbart-Zillerist trend of emphasising the development of a decent nature and the teacher-orientation of the teaching.[150]

American John Dewey (1859–1952) founded the New School movement at the end of the 1890s. Similar attempts at reform appeared in Europe at the start of the 1990s and were known in Finland as the free school (vapaa koulu), the work school (työkoulu), and the active school (aktiivikoulu). The New School aimed to bring perception, initiative, and practical learning to lessons. It tried to move teaching away from a focus

---

145 Hyyrö 2006; Iisalo 1989; Paksuniemi 2009.
146 Koskenniemi 1946, 40.
147 Iisalo 1989, 161–162.
148 Iisalo 1989, 236–237; Paksuniemi 2009, 83–87.
149 Kuikka 1991, 89; Lahdes 1961, 45–46, 67.
150 Bruhn 1968, 10, 12, 31, 62, 207; Iisalo 1989, 200–203; Käis 1937, 45–46, 71–72; Lahdes 1961, 28, 42, 82, 98, 146, 158–159.

on the teacher to a focus on the students, from a lecturing style to working together. Indeed, the principles of the New School were pupil initiative and individuality.[151]

In the 1910s in Finland, there were already New School, or reform pedagogy, ideas popping up, which many primary school teachers tried in practice in the 1920s and 1930s[152]. There were various names for the New School approach. It was called the school of life (elämänkoulu), the school of experience (elämyskoulu), and even experience pedagogy (elämyspedagogiikka). The New School highlighted national and socialist requirements, among other things. The significance of exercise and the environment were also emphasised, as well as individual classroom society.[153]

In the New School, teaching focused on the active pupil, who was free to act according to his or her nature. The teacher was to remember individuality and the requirements of society. In teaching, he or she was to highlight the needs of life outside of school. The New School was considered a work and community school, which aimed to utilise the pupil's own resources. Study had to be down to earth and practical, and the pupil had to be allowed to work independently. The pupil was allowed to set his or her own goals, search for the necessary tools, and plan how to attain the goal himself/herself. In the New School, information had to be useful, self-sought information. Initiative was emphasised for all activities because children were considered to be active by nature. Teaching was to highlight the pupil's sociality, independent initiative, and the needs of society. The diversification of teaching and increase in the pupils' freedom strove to reduce bad behaviour.[154]

Herbartian pedagogy was still visible in the 1921 College Committee Report (Seminaarikomiteanmietintö). The curriculum at teacher training colleges was constructed with the aim that individual development and education would follow the overall development of mass education.[155] The

---

151 Halila 1950, 72; Heikkinen 2003, 137; Käis 1937, 5–6, 29; Lahdes 1961, 42, 62, 90–92, 130.
152 Somerkivi 1979, 173.
153 Peltonen 1989, 101–102.
154 Hyyrö 2006; Paksuniemi 2009; Valta 2002.
155 Kuikka 1973, 118, 237.

educational ideas of the New School were not accepted by the teachers at the Finnish teacher training colleges as they had learned the Herbart-Zillerist way of thinking and were not ready for the change. First of all, the teachers at the teacher training colleges in Finland had graduated from the Finnish colleges where teaching was carried out according to Herbart-Zillerism.[156] Secondly, the textbooks that were used in the teacher training colleges were rarely changed[157]. The Herbart-Ziller methodology remained the unofficial guiding principle of Finnish teacher training till 1940s, and therefore of the entire primary school system[158].

4.2. The teacher training college of Tornio

Cygnaeus believed that teacher training in Finland should invest in women, since as carers of small children, women would influence the overall intellectual development of the people. In a letter from 1874, he wrote that the most important matter in his homeland, increasing the people's intellect and decency, takes place through investing in educating women and through improved childcare and education. In 1880, he clarified:

"The true starting point and core of mass education must be better female education, which in turn reforms home education."[159]

Women were seen as being better suited than men to teach young children, as the children needed maternal care. The liveliest older children required control which a female teacher could not necessarily give. Cygnaeus saw women as the educators of society. On the basis of this idea, the establishment of female colleges was planned. Cygnaeus believed that students at female colleges should be selected from some of the most educated homes in the country. This did not mean that he underrated the common people. On the contrary, Cygnaeus demanded respect and appreciation for all women. He defended upper-class women as the most suitable educa-

---

156 Loukola 1926; OMA, TSeA, Ba:1.
157 OMA, TSeA, Dd:1.
158 Lahdes 1961, 70–71.
159 Cygnaeus 1910, 31, 44, 85.

tors, for example, by arguing that after becoming teachers, these women could easily obtain the necessary respect.[160]

The training of primary education teachers was developed at the end of the 1860s, but teaching could not be given to all educators of young children and teaching varied quite widely[161]. In Finland, teachers have been trained for a long time and the development of teacher training is connected to the development of the school system. In the 1910s, the state took on the responsibility of primary school teacher training, and in 1917, the Chief Director of the Educational Administration Board, Mikael Soininen, proposed the establishment of a 2-year teacher training college for lower primary school teachers.[162]

At the end of the 19th century, the teaching profession became an important career path for women in rural areas since it was now possible to apply for teacher training from outside of urban areas. Indeed, the majority of applicants for Finnish primary school teacher training were from rural areas, where they were also placed to work.[163] Wages depended on gender: a female teacher earned less than a male teacher[164]. Municipalities deliberately saved money in hiring women as teachers. Snellman was convinced that the establishment of teacher training colleges would allow for an increased quality in the level of teaching in Finland. Cygnaeus believed that there should be strict discipline and order in these colleges. Cygnaeus stated that college students should adopt the following attitude:

"May the college aim to awaken in the students a religious mood and a solemn understanding of the important calling of a primary school teacher, but also prevent pride and arrogance."[165]

In 1922, the College Committee stated the following concerning teaching in teacher training colleges:

"The aim of the teaching given in colleges is to help students to form a Christian-decent worldview, to develop them into strong and decent-

---

160   Ibid., 31, 44, 85, 90.
161   Merciful Decree of Imperial Majesty [Armollinen Ohjesääntö]1866.
162   Halila 1950; Hyyrö 2006; Kuikka 1978; Melin 1980; Nurmi 1989.
163   Halila 1963, 271; Rinne 1989, 84.
164   Markkola 1994, 159.
165   Cygnaeus 1910, 201–202.

natured individuals. And to awaken and nurture in them a love for their prospective task, and to give them the required common as well as professional skills and information for their future work. And to develop in them the ability and effort to progress in these and to generally enrich their own emotional being."[166]

During the period of autonomy (1809–1917), a total of eight teacher training colleges were established in Finland[167]. The training of primary school teachers in Finland began relatively late in comparison to Sweden, Norway, Denmark, Switzerland, and Germany. In those countries, mass education and teacher training had generally begun at the start of the 19th century.[168] In Sweden, the teacher training system had been closely connected to the church since it had been established in 1842[169]. In Sweden, teacher training was a 4-year process at the start of the 20th century. In Denmark and Norway, teacher training lasted for 3 years.[170] In the United States, teacher training colleges were popular until the end of the 1920s[171].

Criteria were set for the colleges; for example, a college must be located in the countryside and had to be a boarding school for both men and women, even though the units functioned as separate departments within the same school premises. A separate Training school, a model school, where prospective teachers could practice teaching was to be built for practical studies. All teacher training colleges were built according to the same structure.[172]

There were several reasons for establishing a college at Tornio in 1921. First, there was a need for preserving teachers to countryside. The foundation of the college was connected to regional policy as well as the need for teachers in Northern Finland. One of the goals was to preserve the Finnish language in the school system, as Tornio was located next to the Swedish

---

166 College Committee Report [Seminaarikomiteanmietintö] 1922, 228.
167 Heikkinen 1995, 394; Hyyrö 2006, 200; Nurmi 1989, 19–20; Nurmi 1995, 45, 54, 62, 68, 119, 127, 139, 146.
168 Heikkinen 1995, 388.
169 Enlund 1993, 5, 12, 15.
170 Nurmi 1995, 157–158.
171 Green 1992.
172 Cygnaeus 1910, 21; Halila 1949b, 326; Nurmi 1966, 23.

Picture 1. The teacher training college of Tornio[173].

border and there was already a teacher training college for Swedish-speaking persons. The foundation of the college represented an important chance for women in Northern Finland to have an occupation and for the children to receive an education.[174]

---

173 OMA, TSeA, Ia.
174 Paksuniemi 2009, 39–40.

5. The first steps toward professionalism

After the Finnish Civil War, there were attempts to unify the values of Finnish citizens using the school system. Teachers embodied values that, in turn, unified the people.[175] Teachers were selected for this demanding task according to certain criteria. The following were required of those applying to the first year of a female teacher training college:

1) Is 17 years of age or will turn 17 before the end of the calendar year,
2) has been vaccinated and has attended confirmation class,
3) has attended upper primary school, and
4) has musical tendencies and a healthy physique as certified by a doctor.[176]

Although there was no mention of an upper age limit for college applicants, in practice, those who were 30 years of age were considered to be too old[177]. In 1922, the college committee considered lowering the minimum age limit to 15, but as the minimum age for working as a qualified teacher was 20 years, the committee was satisfied with 17 years. It set an upper age limit of 22 years, when people's thoughts were at their most productive.[178] The aim was to select a group of a certain age for the college so that it would be possible to influence their teacher image[179]. The acceptance criteria for the male teacher training college were very similar. The applicant had to have attended confirmation class, be at least 18 years of age, an upstanding and healthy young man, and proficient in at least the knowledge and skills taught in upper primary school. The applicant was also expected to have a good reputation and references from a member of

---

175 Rantala 2005, 209–210.
176 Temporary Rule of Order [Väliaikainen järjestelysääntö] 1918.
177 OMA, TSeA, Da:1.
178 College Committee Report [Seminaarikomiteanmietintö] 1922, 53–55.
179 See Hyyrö 2006, 256.

society outside of the college. The applicant had to demonstrate that he was well-behaved and honest in entrance examinations.[180]

The least amount of applications (98) to the college of Tornio were sent in 1921, which is probably because the college had just been founded. It took several years to achieve its place among other colleges in Finland.[181] The amount of the applications increased until the year 1932 (203), and the reason for a lower number of applications to all the colleges in Finland during the 1930s was the worldwide economic crises, which caused reductions in the Finnish school system. A bill was proposed to reduce the lower primary school teacher vacancies, but it did not pass. As a result of this, women did not apply for colleges that might not be able to provide work for them.[182] After awhile the number of the applications began to quickly increase; for example, in 1943, 875 applications were sent to the college at Tornio[183]. This high number can be explained by the changes in the society and in school policies. From 1939 to 1945, Finland participated in the Second World War, and in the 1940s, there were only two functioning lower primary school teacher training colleges. One was located in South-West Finland, in Vaasa, and was for Swedish-speaking students only. The other one was in Tornio. Therefore, the teacher college of Tornio was the only possible place to study to become a lower primary school teacher for Finnish-speaking women.[184]

The application process for teacher training colleges in Finland was comprised of two stages—submitting an application to the college and taking entrance examinations[185]. For the entrance examinations, applicants were asked to demonstrate their skills in various subjects. These examinations could last for several days. The board of teachers then selected those applicants who were seen as most suitable to working as lower pri-

---

180 Heikkinen 1995, 395. See Rinne 1989, 174–175.
181 Paksuniemi 2009.
182 Hyyrö 2006, 280–281; Rinne 1973, 128.
183 OMA, TSeA, Bb:1.
184 Hyyrö 2006, 138, 203–204, 252; Paksuniemi 2009, 65–66, 68.
185 OMA, TSeA, Ca:1; Ca:2; Bb:1. See Halila 1949a; Halila 1963, 84; Rinne 1989, 84.

mary school teachers as trial students.[186] The trial student period lasted from 6 months to 1 year. During this period, the student was required to demonstrate good behaviour and to excel in his or her studies. After the trial period was over, it was possible to become a permanent student.[187] In a decree from 1919, the trial period was applied to all teacher training colleges in Finland,[188] which meant that during the first academic year, the student's disposition and characters, as well as their behaviour, were evaluated[189].

During the entrance examinations, a health examination was also carried out, in which a doctor gave his or her own evaluation of the applicant's features:

"Was there anything that you noticed during the examination, or are otherwise aware of, which could be of significance when evaluating the subject's suitability for teaching? Based on this, do you consider the subject you have examined to be suitable for work as a teacher with regard to health, or, if not, on what grounds do you base your evaluation?"[190]

Doctors were expected to examine the applicant from other perspectives than simply their health. One of the students recalled:

"The doctor didn't want to accept me as a student. He taught that I was too weak and tiny to manage through the study years. I assured him that even though I was tiny I had what it took to be a teacher."[191]

The strict evaluation given by the doctor was seen as a preliminary stage for the entrance examinations. The doctor's statement could prevent an applicant from ever reaching the college. The high numbers of graduates from the Finnish teacher training colleges indicate that accepted students fulfilled the stringent criteria set by the college to prepare the students for future work as a teacher and that the students were motivated to graduate. Any interruptions to studies were recorded in annual reports, which were read by not only students and teachers at a college, but were

---

186 See Hyyrö 2006; Paksuniemi 2009.
187 OMA, TSeA, Ae:2. See Hyyrö 2006, 283–290; Paksuniemi 2009.
188 Teacher Training College Act [Seminaariasetus] 1919.
189 Simola 1995, 250. See Rinne 1986b, 132.
190 OMA, TSeA, Ee:21.
191 OMA, TSeA, Cow book 2 [Lehmäkirja 2], 26.

also sent to other colleges in the country and to the National Board of General Education.[192]

The students at the Finnish teacher training colleges were mainly from middle class and farm families in rural areas. This can be partially explained because in Finnish society, the eldest son in a family usually inherited the family farm, so daughters had to plan for their future in a different way. Training to become a lower primary school teacher was one such option. In addition, most of the students who graduated as lower primary school teachers went to work in primary schools in rural areas, as there was a shortage of teachers in these locations. A teacher who grew up in the same environment as the school found it easier to relate to the village community. The fact that the teacher was also familiar with the children's background facilitated his/her work.[193] In Finland, the quality of life and industrial production increased during the 1930s,[194] and the shift from an agricultural to an urban society was visible in the backgrounds of the students studying at teacher training colleges[195].

It was a great honour to be accepted into the college. One of the students who applied to the college reminisced in the archive source The Cow book (Lehmäkirja):

"When we were gathered together to the college hall to hear who were accepted as students to the college. I heard my name and I burst into tears. Then one girl next to me comforted me: Don´t cry. I don´t cry, neither I got in. Another girl said: she doesn´t cry because of that, she cries because she got in! To get accepted into to college was the biggest future solution of my life at that time. My other option was to be a cafeteria musician in a small town. It would have been a really uncertain profession for me."[196]

The number of graduates indicates that the Finnish teacher training colleges were very efficient educational institutions and that their selection process was successful. The close screening of applicants helped to ensure

---

192 OMA, TSeA, Bb:1; Ca:1; Ca:2. See Heikkinen 1995, 422.
193 See Heikkinen 1995, 406; Kaarninen 1995, 207; Paksuniemi 2009; Rinne 1989, 76, 79–83, 110, 193; Valta 2002, 120.
194 Alapuro 1987, 78–83, 86–87, 92–94, 97; Karisto et al. 1988, 31.
195 Alestalo 1977, 101–102; Kerkelä 1982, 50, 198.
196 OMA, TSeA, Cow book 2 [Lehmäkirja 2], 2.

Picture 2. Students and teachers of the teacher training college of Tornio in the 1930s[197].

that the students were suitable, gifted, and most probably motivated to become teachers. Reasons for discontinuing studies were illness, family reasons, poor success at school, or behaviour that was deemed unsuitable for a teacher. In addition, an individual who was unable to learn the skills and knowledge required of a lower primary school teacher was not allowed to graduate.[198]

---

197 OMA, TSeA, Ia.
198 Annuals 1925–1945; OMA, TSeA, Bb:1; Ca:2; Ca:3; Da:1.

6. The development of the teacher personality

6.1. Emphasis of academic subjects

The curricula of the teaching training college of Tornio consists academic subjects such as Didactics, Religion, Finnish language, Enviromental Studies, Maths and Helth Education. The textbooks used in the academic subjects instructed prospective students on organising teaching, knowledge of the subjects, and the use of various materials, on which reforms brought by the New School ideology also had an effect. Textbooks emphasised different personal characteristics, such as following a calling and carrying out one's work happily, taking initiative and working for the good of one's pupils, living a simple life with a healthy lifestyle, being a teetotaller and physically active, and having a decent, clean personality. Teachers were not allowed to go dancing or to the theatre. Pietilä points out: "Teacher's decent activity included that the teacher abstains from going to dancing or to theatre and acts in a teetotal and decent manner". These demands covered teacher's free time also because teachers were role models.[199] Teachers also had to be decent during their free time. They had to be tactful, hard-working, and educated; speak in the manner of an educated person; dress neatly; and have flawless handwriting.[200] According to Salmela, teachers' should be teachers during their free time also: "The teacher's participation in the local spiritual occasions, temperance and juvenile work, and economic hobbies offers in many ways the best chance to create the connection of appreciation and sympathy between the home and school"[201].

---

199 Pietilä 1928, 3–5.
200 E.g., Boxström 1900, 149–150, 160–161; Ottelin 1931, 75, 98, 105, 153, 164–166; Salo 1924, 25, 147, 155–161; Soininen 1911, 85, 94, 195.
201 Salmela 1931, 153.

Teachers had to be of a Christian nature and maintain his or her Christianity by being an active member of the parish and by engaging in cooperation with the parish. The teacher had to be familiar with the content of the *Bible*, the *Hymnal*, and the *Catechism*. For example Boxtröm defines:"Teaching affects strongly children's religious emotions if it comes from the heart of a religious teacher and is based on the consistent religious conception of the world"[202]. Soininen builds teacherhood on Christianity when he highlights: "Love your neighbour as you love yourself"[203]. The teacher had to be patriotic and proud of his or her homeland, familiar with the basic works of national poetry and Finnish literature, and knowledgeable of Finnish nature and rural areas[204]. For example Salo notes: "The one who has attached to his/her home and home district already in his/her childhood can love his/her great common home, that is his/her native country, when grown-up"[205]. Soininen points out: "A patriotic celebration may arouse noble enthusiasim"[206]. According to Salo teacher's task beside teaching was to take care of arousing social, decent and religious feelings in pupils[207].

6.2. Playing the harmonium and singing

The students of the teacher training college practised playing the harmonium for half an hour every day in special playing booths. Every week, they had to demonstrate their skill for 15 to 20 minutes. At the same time, the teacher gave new instructions on playing the harmonium to the student.[208] This was one way to ensure that the students kept up with the requirements. Students who had played before began with more difficult songs,

---

202 Boxtröm 1900, 5.
203 Soininen 1911, 2.
204 E.g., Boxtröm 1900, 149–150, 160–161; Ottelin 1931, 75, 98, 105, 153, 164–166; Salo 1924, 25, 147, 155–161; Soininen 1911, 85, 94, 195. See Lahdes 1961, 80.
205 Salo 1928, 14–15.
206 Soininen 1923, 26.
207 Salo 1926; Salo 1928.
208 Annuals 1921–1945; OMA, TSeA: Dd:1.

and the ones who had not played before studying started from the basics. The aim was to achieve a certain playing level so that when the student started her work as a teacher, she could accompany songs and hymns. Cygnaeus even suggested that students who could play the harmonium well could accompany hymns at the church services.[209] The students practiced playing with different song books depending on their skills[210]. The requirements were the same at every teacher training college in Finland[211].

The music teacher would tell the student when she played well enough and could accompany a hymn during the morning service: "You had to keep your end up in that accompaniment of morning hymn"[212]. This was something that the students looked forward to. The students could also demonstrate their skills at college parties, where they could accompany songs that were sung together as a group. This kind of activity was good practice for work as a teacher. The students were taught how to take care of the harmonium. This was a very important skill because the instrument was very expensive, and taking good care of it made it last longer. The other reason was that the schools in the countryside were located in such remote locations that it was difficult to get anyone to fix the harmonium if it was broken.[213]

Teaching and learning how to sing was based on Cygnaeus' requirement: the practice of teaching singing should increase a student's religious, morality, and aesthetic feelings. They should practise their skills by singing at church, schools, and homes, and they should also sing patriotic folk songs.[214] This also applied to the teaching at the teacher training colleges in Tornio. During singing lessons, students learned theory and sang children's songs, hymns, spiritual songs, and national songs. In their lessons, they used song books and the hymnal, and once a week, they had a choir practice lesson. The lyrics of the songs included Christian, patriotic, and

---

209 Cygnaeus 1910, 247.
210 Annuals 1921–1945; OMA, TSeA: Dd:1.
211 OMA, TSeA, Dd:1. See Hyyrö 2006; Nurmi 1995; Paksuniemi 2009.
212 OMA, TSeA, Cow book 2 [Lehmäkirja 2].
213 Annuals 1930–1939; OMA, TSeA, Dd:1.
214 Cygnaeus 1910, 245–246.

moral themes.[215] The choir performed at different events at the college, in the surrounding area, and at the local church[216].

The teachers at the college tried to pass on all their knowledge that students would need for work as teachers. Practicing playing and accompanying songs, along with learning different songs and singing and leading the choir, were excellent tools for the future.

Picture 3. The choir wearing Finnish traditional costumes made by themselves[217].

6.3. Practical skills for life

In their handicraft lessons, students practised knitting, sewing, making dolls, and making fishing nets, fixing old clothes, and making new clothes. They also practised different kind of handicrafts that were focused on teaching the pupils at their future school. Students in the upper classes made traditional Finnish costumes, which took a long time to finish.[218] Class time was not sufficient to complete these projects, which meant that

---

215   Annuals 1921–1930; OMA, TSeA, Ae.2; Ae:19.
216   Annuals 1939–1945.
217   OMA, TSeA, Ia.
218   Annuals 1921–1945; OMA, TSeA, Ae:2; Dd:1; Dd:3.

the students had to do extra work during their spare time. Sewing the traditional costumes was a demonstration of the importance of Finnish culture and national traditions. Beginning in the 1930s, the students were taught how to make Finnish national flags.[219] The instructions were given in a didactics book[220] and met the patriotic education requirements that were set for mass education and were in place in teacher training. The activities during the lessons and the books that were used were similar to the ones that were used at different teacher colleges in Finland.[221]

Picture 4. The students with the dolls made by themselves in 1931[222].

The didactics textbooks gave instructions on how to teach handicrafts to the pupils but also set out requirements for the teacher image. For example, they gave instructions on how to speak, how to dress, and how to behave.[223] The lessons at school should be strict and busy rather than playful

---

219 Annuals 1930–1939; OMA, TSeA, Dd:1.
220 Salo 1928, 252.
221 See Hyyrö 2006; Nurmi 1995; Paksuniemi 2009.
222 OMA, TSeA:Ia.
223 Salo 1919, 10–11; Salo 1924, 25, 147, 155–161; Salo 1926, 25, 64–70, 156–160; Salo 1928, 14–15, Salo 1929, 17–18, 45–47, 65–67: Soininen 1911, 85, 94, 195; Soininen 1923, 27, 80–86; Törnudd 1929, 2–4, 7–8; Valve & Tappura 1937, 5–13.

and amusing[224]. This was based on requirements for discipline and order in primary schools[225]. One of the themes in the lessons was saving money[226].

The purpose of the handicraft lessons was to raise students to be hardworking citizens who could use their skills in real life, such as sewing clothes for themselves and their families, mending old clothes, and using recycled materials[227]. Saving was an important skill from 1921 to 1945 because of the global economic depression. The economic depression first affected the United States and Germany, and England and the Nordic countries were not quite so badly affected. However, the effects of the depression were felt in Finland, especially in the educational sector.[228] In 1939, war broke out and lasted until 1945. There was a lack of food and other materials during the years studied in this paper.[229]

Teaching handicrafts was based on Cygnaeus's idea that handicraft skills were a part of a civilized nation and part of regular family life. A skilled and hardworking person was useful[230]; this idea was also emphasised in the New School ideology[231]. The archive sources also point out that students were not only required to achieve good skills, but also to acquire knowledge on how to teach children these skills. Another goal was to pass on practical knowledge for life as a woman. Furthermore, this thinking was based on the Herbart-Zillerist ideology in which citizens should be raised to be moral and skilled in various aspects.[232]

---

224 Törnudd 1929, 2–4, 7–8.
225 Valta 2002.
226 Salo 1928, 149.
227 Bruhn 1968, 36–37; Heikkilä 2008, 161–171; OMA, TSeA, Dd:1; Tuomaala 2004, 224.
228 Heikkinen 1995, 236; Rinne 1973, 128; Virrankoski 1975, 194–195.
229 Rinne 1973, 128; Virrankoski 1975, 194–195.
230 Cygnaeus 1910, 181–183
231 Bruhn 1968, 36–37.
232 E.g., Iisalo 1989; Lahdes 1961.

6.4. Gymnastics, games, and sports

During physical education lessons, the students practised different kinds of sports. They did gymnastics and learned different games and songs that they could teach the pupils. They were taught how to play Finnish baseball and how to ski. The books that were used during the lessons were didactic books and meant for teaching children. They contained precise instructions on how to teach children.[233] As not every school had a gymnasium, some of the instructions were planned for "desk gymnastics,"[234] meaning that the pupils would use their desks during the exercise period. This demonstrates the value placed on exercise. Traditional Finnish songs and folk dances were practiced in the lessons. One goal was to learn Finnish folk dances, thereby incorporating Finnish traditions into the lessons and promoting patriotism.[235] It was very important for the college students to learn all the movements correctly so that they could teach the pupils and show their skills in different events at the college.

Picture 5. Students of the college performing gymnastics in the 1940s[236].

---

233 Annuals 1921–1945; Björkstén 1920, 9, 177, 193–194; Björkstén 1926; Collan 1908, 1, 14; Collan 1921, 14; Collan 1922, 35–37; OMA, TSeA, Dd:1; Stenroth 1923, 8–15; Stenroth 1929.
234 Stenroth 1923, 8–15; Stenroth 1929.
235 See Halila 1963; Isosaari 1961.
236 OMA, TSeA, Ia.

The physical training also had a deeper goal: "The meaning of gymnastics was to improve the body and soul." The didactic book also included guidelines for the teacher image: "Teachers should be talented, always happy, precise and fair."[237] The teachers were also expected to be kind, glad, cheerful, and energetic[238]. These requirements were typical for Herbart-Zillerism, which claimed that education aimed at wholeness and growth of both the body and soul[239]. The textbook recommended cheerful folk songs and dances instead of ceremonious patriotic songs to accompany gymnastics. As such, patriotism was not removed from lessons, but changed into an emphasis on Finnish culture and traditions. The same phenomenon was seen in musical games and in folk dances, where emphasis was placed on Finnish dances.[240]

In Finland, female sports were a relatively new concept in the 1910s and were faced with prejudice[241]. These prejudices seem to have grown weaker by the end of the 1930s, however, when teacher training colleges began to use two books relating to the topic. Indeed, sport was a visible feature in Finnish culture in the 1930s. Skiing skills were improved at teacher training colleges. New sports taught in the physical education lessons were Finnish baseball and orientation, which were recommended forms of group activities.[242] During these lessons, students were made familiar not only with new forms of exercise but also with civil defence instructions as Finland's foreign affairs situation was growing tense toward the end of the 1930s. The basics of orientation were learnt during skiing lessons.[243]

According to textbooks, the purpose of the active and diverse exercise was to raise lively citizens. Carrying out exact gymnastic movements also taught the disciplined following of rules. A lively and obedient citizen was an efficient member of civic society. Learning folk dances was education in Finnish culture. As such, exercise was embraced as part of turning

---

237 Björkstén 1920, 9, 177, 193–194. See Koivusalo 1982, 61.
238 Kallio 1916, 7–8.
239 Iisalo 1989, 236–237; Lahdes 1961, 28–32.
240 Annuals 1930–1945; OMA, TSeA, Dd:1.
241 See Koivusalo 1982, 63.
242 Annuals 1921–1945; Käis 1937, 97; OMA, TSeA, Da:2.
243 Annuals 1939–1945.

students into upstanding citizens.[244] Another motive of teaching Finnish gymnastics was to awaken nationalism and to emphasise and protect the love of one's country[245].

---

244 See Tuomaala 2004, 239–240.
245 Koivusalo 1982, 107–108.

7. Process factors that strengthen the teacher image

7.1. Practical training at the Training school

The teacher was the most important motivator and keeper of the peace in the classroom. The kind of teaching he or she had received during teacher training, the place where the teaching was carried out, the size of the class, and curricula from which the teacher taught were all important factors relating to the success of the teaching. Discipline had to originate from the teacher himself, as he or she had to maintain strict and consistent self-discipline in either his or her presentation and own thoughts. The teacher had to ensure peace with his or her personality, calmness, and, most of all, his or her fair approach. A true teacher was considered to be a person who placed high expectations upon himself. A large factor was how well the teacher knew his or her pupils in order for him to be able to read the behaviour of the pupils. The teacher had to have a diverse understanding of his or her pupils' natures, tendencies, and habits. In addition, the teacher had to form his or her approach to discipline in accordance with each pupil's nature; that is, he or she had to pay attention to individuality. This was not just applicable to the classroom; rather, the teacher also had to monitor the pupils during breaks and on excursions. Finnish teacher training institutions strove to teach these qualities to their prospective primary school teachers. This was the foundation from which pedagogy in Finnish teacher training colleges was carried out.[246]

A primary school teacher was expected to carry out his or her work industriously for the good of the children, thereby gaining the respect and trust of the parents. The greatest responsibility for this lay with the teachers, who were to demonstrate that they were genuinely working for the good of the children with their own behaviour. Teachers were expected

---

246 Halila 1949b; Paksuniemi 2009; Tuomaala 2004; Valta 2002.

to be up-to-speed and aware of what was going on in the school environment.[247] They were to go on home visits even when there was no problem that needed to be addressed. Parents were to be invited to the school to discuss matters relating to their children's attendance at school. Various celebrations and events had to be organized with a focus on the parents in order to improve cooperation. In addition to these events, parent-teacher meetings were organized, during which parents and teachers were to discuss, socialize, and hold relevant presentations. The school may have organized special days focusing on the home life outside of school. In addition, the school was to organize special mother, father, and parent days.[248] The success of cooperation required mutual trust, respect, and understanding. The school and the home had to have a common goal: the education and teaching of the child. The home had to accept the fact that teachers acted in place of parents at school.[249] Requirements for the teacherhood were noticed during the teaching practice.

During their studies, students completed a period of teaching practice at the Training school. They observed six lessons held by the practice school teachers each week. In the spring term, they still observed six lessons a week, but also taught practice lessons in the Training school classes themselves. The practice period lasted from 2 to 3 weeks. The college students were instructed in the planning of teaching, the use of questions and observational tools in teaching, and in various teaching methods. Students were taught how to bring teaching down to the children's level.[250] This pupil-oriented approach was a change brought by the New School ideology in 1930s[251].

The importance of the teacher's own personality was emphasised in teaching, and the didactics for various subjects were reviewed[252]. A teacher from the college and training school observed the lessons held by the students and gave feedback either after the lesson or at some other agreed

---

247 Mäntyoja 1951, 220–221.
248 See Säntti 2003.
249 Etelälahti 1920, 45–47.
250 OMA, TSeA, Ae:28.
251 See Kuikka 1991, 89; Lahdes 1961, 45–46, 67, 99.
252 OMA, TSeA, Ae:28.

time. The feedback session was similar to a consultation.[253] Feedback sessions concentrated on the lesson taught by the student and his/her role as a teacher. The student had to be in control of the discipline and order in the classroom. They were warned against pretence, as the pupils at the Training school were able to distinguish genuine and insincere behaviour. During the practice period, attention was paid to both the student's pedagogical work and his or her role in the classroom. Student's use of language and tone were evaluated, as the use of dialect was not permitted. In addition, the student's ability to achieve a status of authority in the classroom was also taken into account. Usually pupils in the Training school behaved well and were obedient; there were only problems in one lesson[254]. Paying attention to the teacher in front of the class was based on the idea that the teacher had to be a model example to his or her pupils[255]. The evaluation of teaching was justified as the practice period was the only time when students were able to test their skills as a teacher. They did not gain any normal experience of teaching in a regular school. It was with these skills and experience that they then moved on to face their future pupils.

According to the didactics textbooks, the teacher's entire personality influenced a pupil's concentration, including the teacher's tone, behaviour, dress, and interest in the subject. The teacher had to dress neatly and behave with discretion and had to leave an all-round impression of a civilised and educated person on the pupils and environment.[256] It was very important for the teacher to set an example in front of the pupils. Books also emphasised the influence of the Christian teacher personality and the teacher's outer appearance in front of the class.[257] Encouraging a sense of

---

253 Annuals 1921–1930; College Committee Report [Seminaarikomiteanmietintö] 1922; OMA, TSeA, Dd:1. See Nurmi 1981, 39.
254 OMA, TSeA, Ae:28.
255 Björkstén 1920, 9, 177, 193–194; Boxtröm 1900, 5, 149–150, 160–161; Kallio 1916, 7–8; Palmén & Wilksman 1921, 3–4, 217–223; Salo 1919, 10–11; Salo 1924, 25, 147, 155–161; Salo 1926, 25, 64–70, 156–160; Salo 1928, 14–15, Salo 1929, 17–18, 45–47, 65–67, Soininen 1911, 85, 94, 195; Soininen 1923, 27, 80–86; Törnudd 1929, 2–4, 7–8; Vartia 1931, 168–169.
256 Salo 1929, 116, 146, 155; Törnudd 1929, 2–4.
257 Soininen 1911, 195; Soininen 1923, 59.

admiration and respect from young children was not very difficult, and once this status had been achieved, the teacher had a firm position of authority in the classroom. A child who respected his or her teacher mimicked the teacher's way of speaking, presentation, and even gestures.[258]

The teachers of the college also paid attention to the students' speech. Students at teacher training colleges were aware that all eyes would be on them in their future profession and got a taste of what this was like during the practice period. Teachers at the college dealt with issues relating to the practice period not only in feedback sessions, but also in teacher meetings:

"We discussed the students' lessons in general and decided to inform them as a group of the most common mistakes relating to teach and of flaws concerning discipline and order."[259] Two grades were given for the practice period—one for practical teaching skills and one for practical schooling. The final grade was the average between these two. Evaluation took place on a scale of 1 to 10.[260]

Religious education was one subject taught at the Training school[261]. Requirements concerning religious education in primary schools were drawn up as early as 1866. First-grade pupils were taught *Bible* stories, verses, and hymns through narration. In the second grade, pupils were also taught selected parties of the *Catechism*.[262] *Bible* stories and holidays in the ecclesiastical year were also taught at the practice school, as well as religious songs and hymns relating to ecclesiastical holidays[263]. At the end of the 19th century, the task of religious education was to impart information on basic Christian principles and the history of the Promised Land[264]. These tasks appear to have been current even in religious education in the 1920s. According to the Herbart-Zillerist method, religious education lessons at the Training school began with a story, which was general prac-

---

258 Soininen 1923, 50–51.
259 OMA, TSeA, Ca:1.
260 College Committee Report [Seminaarikomiteanmietintö] 1922; OMA, TSeA, Ca:1; Ca:2.
261 OMA, TSeA, Da:1.
262 Decree on Primary Education [Kansakouluasetus] 1866.
263 OMA, TSeA, Dd:3; De:4.
264 Nurmi 1964, 95–96.

tice in religious education at Finnish primary schools.[265] In environmental studies at the Training school, students utilised what they had learnt at the college by going on excursions with pupils at the Training school to local areas and teaching the pupils about animals. Pupils at the Training school were also taught practical matters, such as going to a shop.[266] These methods indicate that the New School ideology methods were also used in the Training school[267].

For Finnish language lessons, in the first grade at the Training school, an alphabet book was used, with the themes of the book concerning toys, Finnishness, and Christianity[268]. According to Salo, the children's first reading book, the alphabet book, should mirror Finnish thought, emotions, and life. Reading books, on the other hand, should mainly contain works by Finnish authors, folk tales, stories, and poems.[269] Patriotism and Christianity were fairly widespread in the alphabet books and reading books used in Finnish primary schools in the 1920s[270]. The aim of teaching the Finnish language was to develop pupils' literacy skills,[271] which had been a goal since the end of the 19th century[272].

Using skills they had learnt in the college, students taught singing, games, and gymnastics lessons at the practice school[273]. Exercise was to be harnessed as an educational tool. Playing was to take place as a supervised activity that focused on the pupils' optimal development.[274] Pupils practiced various handicrafts in craft lessons at the practice school. The first-grade pupils sewed covers for an alphabet book and crocheted an oven mitten; the second grade sewed a ball and crocheted a bridle. Pupils also practiced handicraft techniques that would be useful in the future, such

---

265 Tamminen 1998, 20.
266 Report of the Primary School Committee [Alkuopetuskomitean mietintö] 1906.
267 See Bruhn 1968, 54–55, 68; Käis 1937, 32, 85, 99–100; Lahdes 1961, 197.
268 Salo 1935, 31–35, 49, 54, 142.
269 Salo, 1929, 132–135.
270 Koski 2001, 31.
271 OMA, TSeA, Dd:3.
272 Nurmi 1964, 96.
273 OMA, TSeA, Dd:3.
274 Tuomaala 2004, 239–240.

as making nets and wickerwork. Toys such as trains or carts were made out of recycled materials.[275] These activities emphasised frugality, which, in turn, was associated with societal decency. Topics that were discussed in the handicraft lessons were selected from the children's environment. Handicraft lessons aimed to teach skills necessary for being a productive citizen. In the Cygnaeus school of thought, work and industry created decent citizenship, and it was the task of both genders to become upstanding citizens.[276] Dewey also emphasised the social significance of handicrafts. Pupils were taught working methods that helped to keep the society afloat. According to him, the school should be the embodiment of an active societal life.[277]

Even at the end of the 19th century, the aim of the artistic subjects was to teach pupils skills and knowledge so that they were able to make and repair utensils in daily life, engage in active exercise, and to sing about their own country and heaven.[278] Pictures drawn on the blackboard were an important addition to the teaching of various subjects, and such drawing was emphasised in teaching guides[279]. Teachers at the teacher training college of Tornio decided in 1928 that students completing their teaching practice were to outline the topic to be learnt in that lesson on the blackboard. They issued this decision so that the Training school pupils' attention to and concept of what was to be learnt would become clearer. The student's drawing on the blackboard was to be completed quickly and erased from the board, or covered, once the pupils began to work. The student's drawing offered the pupils a model, but the aim was not for the pupils to copy the student's drawing, but instead to produce their own work. The student also had to write on the board what the other pupils said if there was time left in the lesson. [280] The use of observational materials was in line with methods used by the New School ideology[281].

---

275 OMA, TSeA, Dd:3.
276 See Heikkilä 2008, 166–167; Tuomaala 2004, 223–224.
277 Bruhn 1968, 36.
278 Nurmi 1964, 96.
279 Salo 1928, 192; Soininen 1911, 193.
280 OMA, TSeA, Ca:1.
281 See Käis 1937, 49, 70; Lahdes 1961, 130.

Pupils at the Training school partially used the same textbooks as students at the college. This gave prospective lower primary school teachers the opportunity to test their skills in practice. The duration of the practice period was short and was the only practice period during which students could get a feel for actual teaching. Students at the teacher training college formed a teacher image based largely on the model and feedback given by teachers at the college and the Training school. One aim of the practice period was to teach prospective teachers how to achieve a status of authority in the classroom, which was practiced during the practice period. The teacher's desk was located at the front of the classroom and on a podium,[282] which emphasised the teacher's presence and authority status in the classroom.

Picture 6. Students at the teaching practise at the Training school in 1940s[283].

An additional advantage of the location of the teacher's desk was that the teacher could observe the pupils all the way to the back of the classroom, as the pupils' desks were lower in neat, orderly rows. The furnishing of the classroom was defined in detail in the textbooks:

"Pupils are to receive daylight from the left-hand side. Double desks are to be arranged in three rows. The row at the back may not be more

---

282 Annuals 1933–1935; Vartia 1931.
283 OMA, TSeA, Ia.

than nine metres from the blackboard or the teacher's podium. The first row could not be too close to the teacher's podium. The teacher's podium has to be sufficiently large to fit the teacher's desk and a chair onto it."[284]

Käis, who focused on the New School ideology, criticised the classroom model in which the teacher sat separated from the pupils, carrying out his or her own work while the pupils sat in straight rows following the teacher's example[285]. A freer seating plan for pupils was part of the New School model, which was not implemented in the Training school.

7.2. Supplementary activities and their impact to the teacher image

Teachers at the teacher training colleges organised supplementary activities for their students outside of the school day, such as morning devotions, Christian Association activities, Fellow Corps (Toverikunta), and scouting. These were the same extracurricular activities at all the teacher training colleges in Finland.[286] According to the College committee, the teaching given at the Finnish teacher training colleges had to focus on the development of a religious mindset and a decent nature[287]. This was realised in morning devotions and in religious holiday events. There was a long tradition of morning devotions in the Finnish school system, and it was considered as part of religious education in schools.[288] By attending morning devotions, the prospective teachers internalised the daily nature and importance of this habit[289]. The devotions consisted of a sermon or speech, a prayer, and a hymn, and were often held by the college head

---

284 Vartia 1931, 26.
285 Käis 1937, 50, 25, 61, 69, 81, 91.
286 E.g., Halila 1949a; Halila 1963; Hyyrö 2006, 330–337; Paksuniemi 2009; Rinne 1989, 194.
287 College Committee Report [Seminaarikomiteanmietintö] 1922.
288 Pyysiäinen 1994, 118.
289 Cygnaeus 1910; Halila 1949b.

or a R.E. teacher. It was a routine that a prayer or a hymn was part of the lunchtime also.[290]

Picture 7. Students during the lunchtime in 1939[291].

Although schools days for college students were long and homework and musical practice took time, students had time left over for association-related activities. In the autumn of 1928, college students founded the Christian Association under the guidance of teachers, and the association's activities began in a promising and lively manner. The aim of the Christian Association was to organise activities based on a common Christian foundation. Almost all college students belonged to the association, and college teachers were also involved. The students elected a chair, a treasurer and a secretary. The association's activities included common meetings and the organisation of worship on Sundays. Participation was voluntary. The Christian Association organised meetings, excursions, and an annual Christmas party. In meetings, association members presented various programme numbers, such as songs, speeches, and recitals, and they invited guests to the college. Meetings were held regularly, even though the number of meetings varied somewhat.[292]

---

290 E.g., OMA, TSeA, Ca:1.
291 OMA, TSeA, Ia.
292 OMA, TSeA, Jb:6.

For its part, the Christian Association helped to further strengthen the students' Christian values. Education toward Christianity was related to the goal of a decent Christian citizen, which is what a lower primary school teacher was expected to be. According to Launonen (2000), one part of the ethical educational thinking in the Finnish primary school between 1863 and 1920 was a religious ethical perspective. In it, religion and morals, God and reason, and Christianity and decency were inseparable from each other. A strong religious foundation was the background to the development of a person's decency.[293]

These same themes were visible in the teaching at the teacher training college and in the extracurricular activities. Participation in the Christian Association's activities was part of a Christian education. Christian activities were highly visible at the teacher training college of Tornio. They were a natural part of the college's activities and could not be separated from the college overall. Christian education seemed to have diverged into an activity that was influenced not only by the education given at the college, but also the education given by the church. The status of Christianity in the college can be explained by religion's strong status in the society and [294] that the teacher image required a foundation of Christian values.[295]

Fellow Corps activities were also organised for students in their free time. According to Fellow Corps' rules, the aim of the association was to achieve a good sense of camaraderie and to widen its members' perspectives in regard to their future activities. The aim was also to encourage national and patriotic enthusiasm based on a religious-decent foundation.[296] Both college students and teachers participated in Fellow Corps activities. According to its rules, Fellow Corps elected a curator and deputy curator from the teachers in the first meeting of the academic year via a closed ballot. They controlled and guided activities in line with the Fellow Corps' rules. Members of the Fellow Corps then elected recreational committees.

---

293 Launonen 2000, 153.
294 See Rinne 1989, 138–142.
295 Boxtröm 1900, 5, 149–150, 160–161; Salo 1919, 10–11; Salo 1924, 25, 147, 155–161; Salo 1926, 25, 64–70, 156–160; Salo 1928, 14–15. See Nurmi 1965; Nurmi 1996; Rantala 2005; Rinne 1986a.
296 OMA, TSeA, Ja:14.

Their task was to take care of the programmes for evening parties and other arrangements. The students took turns participating in the organisation of evening parties, as the members of the recreational committee were elected in alphabetical order.

Evening parties were organised at the Finnish teacher training colleges fairly regularly. Evening parties were sometimes lively celebrations. In such cases, the festivity was usually a holiday of national importance and the programme was designed "to illustrate the significance of the day."[297] Usually there was no school day held on the same day as the party, and instead students were able to concentrate on the party[298]. The organisation of patriotic festivities was an activity in line with nationalism, which simultaneously strengthened the formation of a uniform cultural foundation and allowed prospective teachers to practice organising school parties. Instructions on how to organise celebrations were given in the didactics textbooks.[299] Primary school teachers usually lived in the centre of a village at the school, and they were expected to actively participate in village celebrations[300]. They were full-time teachers all the time.

Fellow Corps' activities were opportunities to practice the systematic organisation of parties with the future teaching work in mind, and the college students were taught important values[301]. Folk dances and round games were one programme number in evening parties organised by Fellow Corps[302]. College students had practiced folk dances and round games in their gymnastics, games, and sport lessons[303]. Although college students were forbidden to dance in public, folk dance activities that took place at the college were permitted. Folk dances and round games were activities that strengthened the national identity. In addition, they emphasised traditions and Finnishness. The learning of folk dances also had a wider-ranging purpose. It prepared future teachers for work outside of the school, for

---

297 OMA, TSeA, Ja:2.
298 OMA, TSeA, Ae:2; Ae:19.
299 Soininen 1923, 27, 80–86.
300 See Säntti 2003, 172–174.
301 See Halila 1963, 300–302; Hyyrö 2006; Kuikka 1973, 253; Nurmi 1965.
302 OMA, TSeA, Ja:3.
303 OMA, TSeA, Dd:1.

the possible direction of club and youth club activities. In addition to the Christian Association and Fellow Corps activities, a third form of extracurricular activities was started, scouting. The scouting principle included the scout oath, which a member took upon joining: "I will love my God and my neighbours, my homeland and mankind while carrying out the scout ideal in my life." The purpose of the scouting movement was to educate members toward decency and good manners and to teach necessary life skills and information.[304]

College students and teachers participated in the scouting organisation's activities, which served as examples of the Herbart-Zillerist emphasis on enthusiasm to learn and try new things. The basic components of the scouting activities—decency, Christianity, and patriotism—were close to the values held by the college and was therefore a suitable fit with the Christian Association and Fellow Corps activities.[305] According to Käis (1937), the scouting activities encouraged initiative, which the New School model recommended[306]. The Old and New School methods were combined in scouting activities, the introduction of which in the 1930s indicated an enthusiasm to try and learn new things, which was a change from the previous decade. Extracurricular activities were supervised by the college teachers and reduced the students' free time, which was preparation for their future responsibilities as a classroom teacher and as an active member of their village.[307]

7.3. Controlling students' free time

Students at the teacher training college were prepared for the role of a teacher from the very start of their studies as well as during their free time. Learning how to achieve a status of authority was an important issue for students aiming to become teachers and was something that they practiced

---

304 Hakonen 1995, 17.
305 Halila 1949a; Halila 1963; Hyyrö 2006; Nurmi 1995; Rinne 1989.
306 Käis 1937, 44–45.
307 Salmela 1935, 153. See Hyyrö 2006; Paksuniemi 2009.

in both official teaching situations and activities that the students undertook in their free time. The teachers at the college paid constant attention to their students' behaviour and their external appearance. Lower primary school teachers were to speak in the manner of an educated person, and the college students were taught how to speak formally. For example, the college teachers decided to pay more attention to the students' way of pronouncing the sound 'd' in all lessons.[308] Formal speech indicated the teacher's status as an educated person and not a commoner. The formal speech model worked as an example for pupils, demonstrating that educated people spoke in an educated manner.[309]

This use of language was also required as part of the teacher image during the student's free time at the college. They were closely monitored, no absences from lessons were allowed, free time was to be spent in such a way that it did not cause absence from the official teaching programme, and activities in free time were expected to support a fastidious teacher image. In a decree stipulating the organisation of primary schools in 1931, it was decided that teachers were to meticulously take care of all tasks assigned to him/her and were to demonstrate impeccable behaviour required of his/her status as a teacher both in and outside of the school.[310]

In the 1920s, dancing was a popular activity and a form of socialising for youth. Going to dances, however, was not seen as a suitable activity for prospective teachers as it did not sit well with the decent teacher image.[311] One student remembered a dancing trip in following way:

"Going to the evening parties and dancing was strictly forbidden. I heard that some girls did go and once I went too. Unfortunately, Soilunen's (who was the doctor of the college at whose house some of the students took a room) domestic help was there and who knew me and told my grandfather. This was how our sins were informed to the manageress too. We were examined. We stood in line behind the door of the chancellery. We were asked in one by one. Then, the whole gang was asking the

---

308 OMA, TSeA, Ca:1.
309 Salo 1929, 14, 18.
310 Nurmi 1979, 161.
311 Nurmi 1995, 216–217.

one who exited the room: What did they say? I had my turn as well. – Even you were there even though you were not allowed to? I cried: - Yes, I was. – Who else was there? – I cannot say! – But you have to! And so I nicely listed the scapegoats, tearfully. Behind the door, I was hauled because I had told the names. I was a great perpetrator. After that, I did not attend those parties during the time I studied at the college."[312]

These girls were not excluded from the college[313]. A reprimand was one of the mildest punishments, while exclusion from the college would be the most severe[314]. However, the practical matter of the prohibition was checked from time to time. For example, at the teacher training college of Raahe, in 1935, the teachers deliberated about whether students should be given the permission to go to restaurants. Teachers made a united decision that going to a licensed restaurant was damaging and dangerous for pupils. Students were therefore barred from the consumption of alcoholic beverages and going to restaurants.[315] One requirement for a teacher was absolute teetotalism[316]. The teetotalism requirement did not prove significantly difficult to follow in female colleges; the breaking of such rules took place more often in male colleges[317].

The teachers of the college were expected to punish a student if she could not follow the rules. The rule of teetotalism was rarely broken, however, and the teachers had to punish only a few students during the entire time that the college was in operation.[318] Two students broke the college rules in the 1940s. One had visited the city hotel with her Swedish friend several times and had alcoholic beverages there. The student's roommate told the teachers that she had not returned her room until during the early morning hours and had Swedish friends as visitors. Another student, for her part, admitted that she had had alcoholic beverages at the

---

312 OMA, TSeA, Cow Book 2 [Lehmäkirja 2], 24.
313 Annuals 1921–1945.
314 Cygnaeus 1910.
315 Nurmi 1996.
316 See Nurmi 1965; Nurmi 1996; Paksuniemi 2009.
317 Annuals 1921–1945; Heikkinen 1995, 438; Manninen 1990, 174; Nurmi 1996, 92; OMA, TSeA, Ca:1; Ca:2; Ca:3; Ca:4.
318 OMA, TSeA, Ca:1; Ca:2; Ca:3; Ca:4.

city hotel but denied drunkenness. The college principal enquired after the matter by phone from the landlady who reported that the student had spent several nights out. She was seen during early hours with three Swedish friends and she did not return home before 8 am, when her fellow student had gone to the college. The teachers decided to expel both students from the college—the first for 11 months, and the other permanently.[319]

At the college of Tornio, smoking was not an issue among the students compared with the men's college of Rauma, where it was a constant problem[320]. Nurmi (1996) stated that at the men's colleges, students were punished more often than at women's colleges. Especially during the Prohibition Law 1919–1932, many male students were caught breaking the law. In addition, the principal of the college of Rauma occasionally received phone calls about the male students' behaviour.[321] After the war years, the control over Finnish college students slowly decreased. The spirit of the times was generally more liberal than before the war years 1939–1945. The change also took place because in the 1940s and 1950s, some of the college students were over 30 years old and veterans of the wars.[322] Students' offences were handled in a more gentle manner as long as veterans of war graduated as teachers—yet some punishments were still given from time to time[323]. During the war, discipline and order had relaxed throughout Finland. Therefore, temperance education became a central theme of education after the war. Drinking problems occurred in many families with veterans. At school, the youth were warned about the dangers of alcohol. The reformed temperance education also aimed at producing more efficient employees. The thought of a civic society included the idea of a citizen participating, sharing, encountering, and taking responsibility for other people and shared issues. Failure in following the required behaviour would lead to public disapprobation. Temperance education had a wider

---

319   OMA, TSeA, Ca:4.
320   Nurmi 1996; Paksuniemi 2009.
321   Nurmi 1996.
322   Syväoja 2004.
323   Nurmi 1996.

meaning—turning the whole nations teetotal, which fall under the educational task of improving public health.[324]

Prospective teachers were not permitted to participate in political activities in school or outside of the school. The political stigmatisation of primary school teachers caused problems with employment opportunities at the start of the 20th century,[325] and as such, the National Board of General Education issued a reminder that students at teacher training colleges were to remain uninvolved in such activities[326]. A teacher had to be a patriotic, nonpolitical individual. The strict approach of school authorities to political activity was part of the policy for national unification.[327]

For Finnish teacher training colleges, there was often talk of "college spirit," which was associated with nit-picking, close-mindedness, and strict supervision[328]. Heikkinen (1995) specified that college spirit referred to discipline, the acknowledgement of obligations, and a Christian-decent ethos[329]. Teachers were required to display exemplary and flawless behaviour in class and in their free time, and special attention was paid to this at all Finnish teacher training colleges[330]. A primary school teacher lived among the people, but was distinguished by the social and cultural capital gained from his or her education[331]. Regardless of their status—or, indeed, precisely because of their status—teachers were scrutinised by the villagers even during their free time. A teacher's decency and decorum were closely monitored. If a primary school teacher behaved in a manner deemed inappropriate for his or her profession, the villagers reported the teacher to the school inspector.[332] As such, it was justified that college stu-

---

324 Heikkinen 1995; Jurama & Karttunen 1990; Kuikka 1993; Lähteenmäki 2000; Paksuniemi 2009; Tupper 2008.
325 See Rantala 2002.
326 OMA, TSeA, Ca:3.
327 See Rinne 1973, 95; Rantala 2002, 174.
328 Rinne 1989, 179.
329 Heikkinen 1995, 399.
330 See Hyyrö 2006; Nurmi 1995; Paksuniemi; Rantala 2005, 213.
331 Säntti 2003, 174.
332 Jurama & Karttunen 1990, 32. See Heikkinen 1995, 223–226; Lähteenmäki 2000, 136.

dents were taught about the role of a teacher and the related requirements during their years of study.

8. The formation of the teacher image

8.1. The first steps toward professionalism

Students with basic capabilities for work as a teacher, their journey toward professional maturity began when they applied to become a student and were accepted into the college. Student admission comprised a two-phase selection method. In the first phase, the college's board of teachers read application papers and chose a group of students out of hundreds of applicants to take part in entrance examinations. The applicants demonstrated that they met the criteria set for entrance into the college using various proof and certifications—he or she had to be at least 17 years old and had to have attended confirmation class, completed upper primary school, and be physically healthy and musically gifted.

The second selection phase consisted of entrance examinations. They lasted several days, during which prospective students demonstrated their skills in various subjects. The board of teachers selected those applicants who were seen as most suitable for working as lower primary school teachers to become trial students. The trial student phase lasted for 6 months. During this period, the student was to demonstrate good behaviour and success in his or her studies. After the trial period, a student could become a permanent student.

The teacher training college paid plenty of attention to entrance examinations, and the possibility of an applicant being educated as a teacher was evaluated from many perspectives. In Finland, the methods for selecting students for entrance into teacher training were continuously changing, and even today, student selection is considered one of the central development targets in Finnish teacher training development plan[333].

---

333   OPM 2008, 9, 68–69. See Luukkainen 2000, 257–259.

8.2. The development of the teacher personality

The teacher training college provided plenty of stimuli for the development of the teacher personality and for strengthening skills, values, and behaviour. It provided a strong foundation for professional development. Stimuli and models that were taught to the students at the teacher training colleges were influential on the initial development of a student's teacher personality early on in his or her studies. The desired teacher image was reflected in the requirements set for students at the college. Students were required to obediently comply with rules and practices and to maintain their teacherhood presence outside of the school. These requirements were in place at the college, during students' practice periods at the practice school, and during students' free time. A teacher training student was to refrain from attending dances and going to the theatre and was expected to organise activities for village residents outside of the school day in his or her work. The teacher was a mass educator; society needed active citizens in order for it to develop strongly.

The textbooks defined the teacher image: A teacher had to be a decent person; that is, an educated, well-dressed, well-spoken, composed, dutiful, hard-working individual with respect for the authorities. This morality included decency and teetotalism. Teetotalism was also emphasised in society, as can be seen in the Prohibition Law[334]. A teacher also had to be a Christian and patriotic. Patriotism included a love for one's home region and the internalisation of cultural tradition. Finland's independence and the consequences of the Finnish Civil War set uniform requirements for patriotic education. These themes were included in the activities organised by the college, such as Fellow Corps and the Christian Association.

---

334 Prohibition Law [Kieltolaki] 1919.

8.3. Process factors that strengthened the teacher image

Students practiced assuming the role of a teacher and their knowledge of various subjects by working at the practice school connected to the college. Teaching given at the training school and the related practice were one important part of teacher training. The students' progress was followed not only by the training school, but also by teachers at the college, who evaluated the student's success. In their practical work, students applied theory in practice. They practiced lesson planning, preparation, the use of observational materials, and teaching methods. This was an important phase in the process of becoming a teacher. During the practice period, prospective teachers also practiced getting to know their pupils and teaching a normal and a double-grade class.

The supplementary activities that the students undertook in their free time exemplified the skills, values, and behaviour that were emphasised at the colleges. Hobby groups, Fellow Corps, the Christian Association, morning devotions, and scouting all provided the students with a diverse range of stimuli. Finnish cultural ideals and values were made concrete in such activities. Finnishness and Christianity were emphasised in programmes for shared events. The organisation of and participation in such events was largely the responsibility of the students, and such organisation was necessary practice for work as a teacher. These extracurricular activities trained prospective teachers to become culturally active. Students at the colleges were taught to respect authority and to follow the college rules both at school and in their free time. They were expected to study hard and be upstanding citizens. In their free time, students were expected to behave decently—they were not allowed to attend dances or to break rules concerning decency and teetotalism. Students at Finnish teacher training colleges followed these requirements fairly well.

The following features were emphasised in the teaching of practical skills and during the practice period:

- The teacher had to be able to sing and compose hymns and songs emphasising religion and Finnishness. She also had to be able to sing in and lead a choir. In the teaching of singing, handicrafts, and playing musical instruments, the task was to manage the teaching of subjects, chart the students' own skills, and even to provide them with skills for life as a citizen.
- The teacher had to be physically active.
- The teacher had to know how to fix and make clothes.
- The teacher had to be hard-working, calm, lively, thorough and skilled.
- The teacher had to be fair and friendly toward her pupils.
- The teacher's lessons had to be enthusiastic and vibrant.
- The teacher had to be well-spoken and well-dressed because she was seen as a model for the pupils.

9. Conclusion

In this study, as with historical studies in general, reliability is examined using source materials used during the period in question. The sources used were mostly primary sources, which are considered essential due to their reliability.[335] The external criticism of sources evaluates the authenticity of the material used. The large amount of historic material used in this study is genuine and authentic.[336] The study examined Finnish teacher training in light of the teacher image, focusing on student admission, what learning materials were emphasised, and various extra-curricular activities organised by the college. The study has discovered and presented new information not only concerning the formation and change of the teacher image over a period of 20 years, but also regarding the activities of the Finnish teacher training college from a historical perspective.

This research points out what kind of educational philosophies influenced to the foundation of the Finnish school system in 19th century. At the same time it refines the process where the national school system developed to be a school for the whole nation. Uno Cygnaeus was the instructor of the Finnish school system he underlined the pestalozzian way to educate the citizens as individuals. J.V. Snellman was also involved in the process of designing the school. He emphasized intellectual education that was based on discipline and order. The development of public education was influenced by these two factors: discipline and order. In the early years of the Finnish school system there was not a clear educational line. But there were changes when the German Herbart-Zillerism educational system settled in Finnish education at the end of 1890s. According to it the education was supposed to underline morality and enthusiasm towards knowledge, to become an active citizen. Herbart-Zillerism was underlining the

---

335   Kalela 2000, 169–170; Kuikka 2001, 158–161.
336   Kuikka 2001, 166; Paksuniemi 2009.

teacher's role in the classroom. On the side of this, reform pedagogy's new didactical methods gave ideas to teaching. It highlighted learned based education and that learning was supposed to be pleasant to the pupils. Even though the new school brought changes to teaching methods, the Herbart-Zillerism formed a strong base for the Finnish education system.

The influence of the emphases of teacher training from 1921 to 1945 is still felt today. The teacher image that was formed is still influential today, even though many changes have taken place[337]. Change has also occurred in teacher training. In teacher training today, there is a special emphasis on the development of a teacher's pedagogy studies,[338] a stronger connection between theoretical training and practice,[339] and wide-ranging teacherhood.[340] If teachers' workload and sheer quantity of tasks was tough decades ago, then teachers today do not have it any easier. Today Finnish teachers adopt a "modern, superefficient teacher role," with traditional values, but at the same time, they feel that they are in a never-ending cycle of development.[341]

The educational and moral aspect of work as a teacher has traditionally been the foundation for teacher training, but is this foundation crumbling under so much pressure? Although we cannot return to the past, Finnish teacher training, in line with European teacher training, can gain stability from a country's own national cultural tradition and an appreciation of education, learning, and teacherhood. Even today, strong social, ethical, and moral behaviour is a foundation for teacher training in Finland. Nowadays, however, seen with fresh eyes and with new emphases, teacher training is gentler and more tolerant. Teacher training has been very popular since the 1920s. Even though today's entrance examinations have come a long way, interest in a career as a teacher has not waned among young Finns. There were plenty of applicants for the teacher training colleges even during the period when the Tornio training college for lower primary school teachers

---

337 E.g., Jussila & Lauriala 1989; Kemppinen 2007; Kuikka 1993; Lindén 2001.
338 OPM 2001, 13–16.
339 Kosunen & Mikkola 2001.
340 Jussila 2009, 66–69; Lauriala 2000; Niemi 1992; Niemi 1995; Niemi 1998; Niemi & Tirri 1997; Syrjäläinen 1995.
341 Syrjäläinen 2009, 142–147.

was in operation. Although today's entrance examinations and teacher education differ from in the past, the interest in teaching as a career has not faded from Finnish adolescents' occupational dreams.

Resources

Archival sources

OMA, TSeA [Provincial Archives of Oulu, Archives of the College of Tornio].
Ae:2, Luokkapäiväkirjat 1922–1923 [Classroom diaries].
Ae:19, Luokkapäiväkirjat 1929–1930 [Classroom diaries].
Ae:28, Luokkapäiväkirjat 1944–1945 [Classroom diaries].
Ba:1, Viran ja toimenhaltijoiden nimikirjat 1921–1935 [The personal files of officials and employees].
Bb:1, Oppilaiden nimikirjat 1921–1962 [Registers of the students].
Ca:1, Opettajakunnankokousten pöytäkirjat 1921–1928 [The proceedings of teachers'meetings].
Ca:2, Opettajakunnankokousten pöytäkirjat 1928–1936 [The proceedings of teachers'meetings].
Ca:3, Opettajakunnankokousten pöytäkirjat 1936–1945 [The proceedings of teachers'meetings].
Ca:4, Opettajankokousten pöytäkirjat 1945–1950 [The proceedings of teachers'meetings].
Cow Book 2 [Lehmäkirja 2].
Da:1, Kirjetoisteet 1921–1928 [Copies of letters].
Da:2, Kirjetoisteet 1929–1940 [Copies of letters].
Dd:1, Opetussuunnitelmat 1921–1946 [Curricula].
Dd:3, Harjoituskoulun opetussuunnitelmat 1922–1941 [Training school curricula].
De:4, Opetusharjoitteluvuorojen listat 1923–1970 [Teaching practise lists].
Ee:21, Oppilaiksi hyväksyttyjen hakemukset 1938 [Applications of admitted students].
Ia, Valokuvat [Pictures].

Ja:2, Toverikunnan pöytäkirjat 1922–1935 [The Minutes of the Fellow corps].
Ja:3, Toverikunnan pöytäkirjat 1935–1940 [The Minutes of the Fellow corps].
Ja:14, Toverikunnan säännöt 1922–1960 [The rules of the Fellow Corps].
Jb:6, Kristillisen yhdistyksen toimintakertomus 1928–1969 [The Report of the Christian Association].

Acts, decrees and reports

Act on Compulsory Education [Oppivelvollisuuslaki] 1921.
College Committee Report [Seminaarikomiteanmietintö] 1922.
Decree on Primary Education [Kansakouluasetus] 1866.
Decree on School Districts [Piirijakoasetus] 1898.
Law on Physical Punishments [Laki ruumiillisista rangaistuksista] 1914.
Merciful Decree of Imperial Majesty [Keisarillisen Majesteetin Armollinen Asetus] 1889.
Merciful Decree of Imperial Majesty. Concerning primary school teacher colleges in the Grand Duchy of Finland [Armollinen Ohjesääntö. Keisarillisen Majesteetin Armollinen Ohjesääntö kansakoulunopettajain- ja opettajatarseminaareille Suomen Suurruhtinasmaassa.] 1866.
Prohibition Law [Kieltolaki] 1919.
Report of the Primary School Committee [Alkuopetuskomitean mietintö] 1906.
Teacher Training College Act [Seminaariasetus] 1919.
Temporary Rule of Order [Väliaikainen järjestelysääntö] 1918.

References

Ahonen, J. 2002. Eettinen opettaja. -Eettinen vaikuttaja [Ethical Teacher Ethical opinion-leader]. In R. Sarras (Ed.). Etiikka koulun arjessa [Ethics in school days]. Helsinki: Otava, 65–73.

Ahonen, S. 2003. Yhteinen koulu. Tasa-arvoa vai tasapäisyyttä? [A common school. Equality or evenly-matched?]. Tampere: Vastapaino.

Alestalo, M. 1977. Työväenluokan maailmankuva ja työväenliike [The worldview of the working class and working class movement]. In: M. Kuusi, R. Alapuro & M. Klinge. Maailmankuvan muutos tutkimuskohteena [Change in worldview as the focus of research]. Keuruu: Otava, 98–111.

Airaksinen, T.1988. Moraalifilosofia [Moral philosophy]. Juva: WSOY.

Alapuro, R. 1987. Kansa liikkeessä [People in movement]. Helsinki: Kirjayhtymä.

Alapuro, R. 1994. Suomen synty paikallisena ilmiönä 1890–1935 [The birth of Finland as a local phenomenon in 1890–1935]. Hanki ja jää [Snowdrift and ice]. Porvoo: WSOY.

Allardt, E.1986. Uskontososiologia [The sociology of religion]. In: J. Pentikäinen (Ed.). Uskonto, kulttuuri ja yhteiskunta: kirjoituksia uskontososiologian alalta [Religion, culture and society: writings from the field of the sociology of religion]. Gaudeamus. Helsinki: Kyriiri Oy, 32–46.

Annuals 1921–1945. Tornio.

Antikainen, A., Rinne, R. & Koski, L. 2000. Kasvatussosiologia [Educational sociology]. Helsinki: WSOY.

Asp, E. 1969. Uudistuva opettaja [The renewable teacher]. In: Kasvatusopillinen aikakauskirja 1986–1969. [Pedagogical Journal in 1986–1969]: Suomen kasvatusopillinen yhdistys, 65–73.

Atjonen, P.2005. Eettisesti laadukas opetus [Teaching with ethical quality]. In: O. Luukkainen & R. Valli (Eds.). Kaksitoista teesiä opettajalle [Twelve theses for a teacher]. Keuruu: Otava.

Björkstén, E. 1920. Naisvoimistelu. Ensimmäinen osa [Women's gymnastics. Part one]. Helsinki: Otava.

Björkstén, E. 1926. Naisvoimistelu. Toinen osa [Women's gymnastics. Part two]. Helsinki: Otava.

Boxtröm, B. 1900. Kasvatusopillinen sieluoppi [Educational psychology]. Sortavalan kirjapaino.

Bruhn, K. 1968. 1900-luvun pedagogisia virtauksia [The pedagogical trends of the 1900s]. Keuruu: Otava.

Cavonius, G. 1957. Ruotsin ja Tanskan nykyiset koulutusjärjestelmät [The present educational systems in Sweden and Denmark]. Kasvatusopillinen aikakauskirja 1957 [Pedagogical Journal 1957]. Suomen kasvatusopillinen yhdistys [Finlands Educational Association], 22–34.

Collan, A. 1908. Laululeikkejä [Singing games]. Helsinki: Raittiuskansan kirjapaino.

Collan, A 1921. Kurssikaikuja II [Course echos II]. Helsinki: Raittiuskansan Kirjapaino.

Collan, A 1922. Kansantanhuja. Valikoima suomalaisesta Kisapirtistä [Folkdances. A selection from a Finnish Kisapirtti] Helsinki: Kustannusosakeyhtiö Kirjan Kirjapaino.

Cygnaeus, U. 1903. Uno Cygnaeuksen kasvatusopillisia periaatteita [The educational principles of Uno Cygnaeus]. Kansakoulun Lehti [The Journal of Primary School], 123–128.

Cygnaeus, U. 1910. Uno Cygnaeuksen kirjoitukset Suomen kansakoulun perustamisesta ja järjestämisestä [Uno Cygnaeus's writings about the establishment and organization of the Finnish primary school]. Helsinki: Raittiuskansan Kirjapaino.

Etelälahti, E. 1920. Kansakoulu- ja sen työväen asema Suomessa [Primary school and its workers' position in Finland]. Helsinki: Edistys.

Enlund, S. J. 1993. Svenska kyrkan och folkskoleseminarierna 1842–1968 med särskild hänsyn till seminarierna i Uppsala, Härnösand och Göteborg [The Swedish church and teacher training colleges in 1842–1968 focusing on the colleges in Uppsala, Härnösand and Göteborg]. Årsböcker i svensk undervisninghistoria [Yearbook of Swedish History of Teaching]. Vol 173. Uppsala: Reprocentralen HSC.

Estola, E. & Syrjälä, L. 2002. Kutsumus [Calling]. In: H. L. T. Heikkinen & L. Syrjälä (Eds.). Minussa elää monta tarinaa. Kirjoituksia opettajuudesta [Many narratives live in me. Writings about teacherhood]. Helsinki: Kansanvalistusseura, 85–98.

Green, A. 1992. Education and State Formation. The rise of education systems in England, France and the USA. London: Taylor and Francis Ltd.

Haavio, M. H. 1941. Kansakoulun uskonnonopetuksen siveellinen kasvatustehtävä [The moral educational task of religious education in primary schools]. Helsinki: Otava.

Haavio, M. H.1969. Opettajapersoonallisuus [Teacher personality]. Jyväskylä: Gummerus.

Halila, A.1949a. Suomen vanhin kansakouluopettajisto [Finland's oldest primary school teachers]. Helsinki.

Halila, A 1949b. Suomen koululaitoksen historia I osa [The history of the Finnish school system part I]. Turku: Uuden Auran Osakeyhtiön Kirjapaino.

Halila, A 1950. Suomen koululaitoksen historia IV osa [The history of the Finnish school system part IV]. Turku: Uuden Auran Osakeyhtiön Kirjapaino.

Halila, A. 1963. Jyväskylän seminaarin historia [The history of the teacher college of Jyväskylä]. Porvoo & Helsinki.

Hakonen, N. 1995. Partiojohtajan käsikirja [The handbook of a Scout Leader]. Mahdollisuuksia ja vihjeitä. Suomen partiolaiset [The Guides and Scouts of Finland] Finland's Scouter ry. Helsinki: Karisto Oy.

Harris, C.E. 1992. Applying moral theories. Belmont: Wadsworth.

Heikkilä, A. 2008. Vaate lapsen elämässä. Koululaisen pukeutuminen pohjoissuomalaisessa maalaiskylässä vuosina 1909–1939 [Clothes in the life of a child. Clothing of a schoolchild in a countryside village in Northern Finland during the years 1909–1939]. Rovaniemi: University of Lapland.

Heikkinen, H. L. T. 2001. Tarinat ja opettajaksi tulemisen taito. Narratiivisen identiteettityön kehittäminen opettajankoulutuksessa toimintatutkimuksen avulla [Stories and the skill of becoming a teacher. The development of narrative identity work in teacher training through action research]. University of Jyväskylä, Research 175.

Heikkinen, H. L. T. 2002. Tarinat opettajankoulutuksen välineenä [Stories as a tool in teacher education]. In: H. L. T. Heikkinen & L. Syrjälä (Eds.). Minussa elää monta tarinaa. Kirjoituksia opettajuudesta. [Many narratives live in me. Writings about teacherhood] Helsinki: Kansanvalistusseura, 99–100.

Heikkinen, H. L.T. & Huttunen, R. 2007. Opettaja ihmisenä ja ammattilaisena [The teacher as a human and a professional]. In: E. Estola, H. L. T. Heikkinen & R. Räsänen. Ihmisen näköinen opettaja [A teacher that resembles a person]. University of Oulu, E 92, 15–27.

Heikkinen, R. 1995. Kasvatus ja koulutus Kainuussa. Kainuun koulutusjärjestelmän kehitys syyskuuhun 1945 mennessä [Education and schooling in Kainuu. The development of the school system in Kainuu before September 1945]. The Teacher Training Department of Kajaani. University of Oulu.

Heikkinen, R. 2003. Kasvatus eri kulttuureissa [Education in different cultures]. Sipoo: IMDL Oy Ltd.

Heporauta F. A. 1945. Suomen kansakoululaitoksen historia [The history of the Finnish primary school]. 2nd (ed.) Otava: Helsinki.

Herbart, J. F. 1806. Allgemeine Pädagogik aus dem Zweck der Erziehung abgeleitet. [General pedagogy]. Göttingen.

Hilgenheger, N. 1993. Johann Friedrich Herbart (1776–1841). Prospects: The quarterly review of comparative education. International Bureau of Education. XXIII, 3/4, 649–664. Paris: UNESCO.

Hyry, E. K. & Hyvönen, L. 2003. Musiikki opettajan elämässä [Music in a teacher's life]. In: H. L. T. Heikkinen & L. Syrjälä (Eds.). Minussa elää monta tarinaa. Kirjoituksia opettajuudesta [Many narratives live in me. Writings about teacherhood]. Helsinki: Kansanvalistusseura, 64–84.

Hyyrö, T. 2006. Alakansakouluopettajien valmistuksen kehitys Suomessa vuosina 1866–1939 [The development of primary school teacher training in Finland between 1866–1939]. Acta Universitatis Tamperensis 1147. Tampere: University Press.

Isosaari, J. 1961. Jyväskylän seminaarin kasvatus- ja opetusopin opetus vuosina 1865–1901 [The education of the science of education and pedagogy at the Jyväskylä teacher training college in 1865–1901]. College of Jyväskylä, Research XXV.

Iisalo, T. 1989. Kouluopetuksen vaiheita keskiajan katedraalikoulusta nykyisiin kouluihin [The phases of education from the medival cathedral school to modern schools]. Keuruu: Otava.

Jurama, V. & Karttunen, T. J. 1990. Kouluntarkastajat. Sattumia ja ajankuvauksia kahdelta vuosisadalta [The school inspectors. The coincidences and pictures of the time from two centuries]. Valtion Kouluhallinnon Virkamiehet ry. Jyväskylä: Gummerus Kirjapaino Oy.

Jussila, J. 2009. Yliopistollista opettajankoulutusta koskevien valtakunnallisten kehittämispyrkimysten sisällölliset yleistavoitteet. [The content of general goals for national development attempts concerning university teacher training]. In: K. Kurtakko & J. Leinonen & M. Pehkonen (Eds.). Opettajaksi kehittyminen, hyvinvointi ja oppimisen strategiat [Becoming a teacher, strategies for wellbeing and learning]. Rovaniemi: University Press, 58–71.

Jussila, M. & Lauriala, A. 1989. Luokanopettajaksi opiskelevien uranvalintamotiivit, koulutusodotukset sekä koulutus- ja kenttäkokemukset [The motives, expectations and educational and field experiences of the class teacher students]. Research of the Faculty of Education, University of Oulu.

Kaarninen, M. 1995. Nykyajan tytöt. Koulutus, luokka ja sukupuoli 1920 - ja 1930 -luvun Suomessa [Modern girls. Education, class and gender during 1920–1930 in Finland]. Helsinki: The Historical Society of Finland.

Kallio, E.1916. Komentoharjoituksia ynnä liikevaraston luettelo liikesukuihin järjestettynä [A collection of drill and other movement practices grouped by movement]. 3rd (ed.) Helsinki: Otava.

Kalela, J. 2000. Historiantutkimus ja historia [Historical research and history]. 2nd (ed.). Tampere: Tammer-Paino Oy.

Kelsall, R. K. & Kelsall, H. M.1969. The school teacher in England and the United States. London: Pergamon Press.

Kemppinen, L. 2007. Ihannehakijan muotokuva – epävirallinen valintakeskustelu ja opettajuuteen liitetyt uskomukset [The profile of an ideal applicant – unofficial discussion on selection and beliefs concerning teacherhood]. In: P. Räihä & T. Nikkola (Eds.) Sattumia vai osumia? Opiskelijavalinnan olemuksen määrittelyä [Coincidence or not? Defining student admission]. Jyväskylä: PS-kustannus, 185–228.

Kerkelä, H. 1982. Suomen luokka- ja kerrostumarakenteen kehityspiirteitä 1900-luvulla. Vertaileva luokkarakenne- ja luokkatietoisuusprojekti [Development characteristics in Finnish classes and strata in the 1900s. A comparative class structure and awareness project]. Research of Sociology and Social Psychology 47, University of Tampere.

Koivusalo, I. 1982. Voimistelu maamme oppikoulujen oppiaineena vuosina 1843–1917 [Gymnastics as a subject in the schools of our country]. Publication of Finnish Society of Sport sciences 83.

Kosunen, T. & Mikkola, A. 2001. Opettajankoulutuksen tavoitteet ja todellisuus [The aims and reality of teacher education]. Kasvatus [Education] 32, (5), 478–492.

Koskenniemi, M. 1946. Kansakoulun opetusoppi [Didactics of primary school]. Helsinki: Otava.

Koski, L. 1999. Hyvä tyttö ja hyvä poika. Ihanteelliset yksilöt aapisten moraalisissa kertomuksissa [Good girl and good boy. Ideal individuals in the moral narratives of ABC books]. In: T. Tolonen (Ed.). Suomalainen koulu ja kulttuuri. Tampere: Tammer-Paino, 21–49.

Koski, L. 2001. Hyvän lapsen ja kasvattamisen ideaalit. Tutkimus aapisten ja lukukirjojen moraalisen kosmologian muutoksista itsenäisyyden aikana [The ideals of a good child and education. A study of the changes in moral cosmology in ABC books after Finland gained its independence]. Finnish Educational Society. Turku: Painosalama Oy.

Krokfors, L. 1998. Opettajankoulutuksen haasteet [The challenges of teacher education]. In: O. Luukkainen (Ed.). Tulevaisuuden tekijät [Builders of the future]. Juva: WSOY, 82–88.

Kuikka, M. T. 1973. Uskonnonopetus Suomen kansakouluopettajaseminaarissa vuosina 1863–95 [Teaching RE in teacher training colleges during 1863–95]. The Department of Practical Theology. Publication of Religious Pedagogy A 5.

Kuikka, M. T. 1978. Kansakoulunopettajan koulutussuunnitelmien kehitys Suomessa vuosina 1917–1923 [The development of primary school teacher training curricula in Finland 1917–1923]. Publication of the Faculty of Education 4. University of Joensuu.

Kuikka, M. T. 1991. Suomalaisen koulutuksen vaiheet [The stages of Finnish education]. Keuruu: Otava.

Kuikka, M. T. 1993. Opettajakuvan muuttuminen 1940-luvulta 1990-luvulle [The changing of the teacher image from 1940 to 1990]. Finnish Historical School Society yearbook.

Kuikka, M. T. 2001. Kasvatuksen historian tutkimus [Researching the history of education]. Helsinki: Otava.

Kuikka, M. T. 2003. Koulun merkitys Suomalaisen kansallisvaltion ja kansalais-yhteiskunnan kehityksessä [The significance of the school in the development of the Finnish nation state and society]. In: J. Rantala (Ed.). Koulu ja kansalaisyhteiskunta historiallisessa perspektiivissä [School and society from a historical perspective]. Helsinki: Hakapaino, 31–46.

Kujala, J. 2008. Miesopettaja itsenäisyyden ajan Suomessa elokuvan ja omaelämäkerran mukaan [The male teacher during independence in Finland through film and autobiography]. Faculty of Education, The Teacher Training Department E 97. University of Oulu.

Käis, J. 1937. Uuden koulun työtapoja [The New School and its working methods]. Helsinki: Otava.

Lahdes, E. 1961. Uuden koulun vaikutus Suomen kansakouluun [The influence of the New School on the Finnish primary school]. Keuruu: Otava.

Lapinoja, K.-P. 2006. Autonomia ja opettajan ammatillisuus [Autonomy and the teaching profession]. In: A. Eteläpelto & J. Onnismaa (Eds.). Ammatillisuus ja ammatillinen kasvu [Professionalism and professional growth]. Aikuiskasvatuksen 46. vuosikirja. Helsinki: Kansanvalistusseura ja Aikuiskasvatuksen tutkimusseura, 144–161.

Launonen, L. 2000. Eettinen kasvatusajattelu suomalaisen koulun pedagogisissa teksteissä 1860-luvulta 1990-luvulle [Ethical educational thinking in the pedagogical texts of the Finnish school from the 1860s to the 1990s]. Jyväskylä Studies in Education, Psychology and Social Sciences 168. University of Jyväskylä.

Lauriala, A. 1997. Development and change of professional cognitions and action orientations of Finnish teachers. Acta Universitatis Ouluensis E 27. University of Oulu.

Lauriala, A. 2000. Opettajan ammatillinen uudistuminen: sosiokulttuurinen näkökulma opettajan oppimiseen [The reform of the teaching profession: a socio-cultural perspective on teacher learning]. In: K. Harra (Ed.). Opettajan professiosta [On the teaching profession]. Helsinki: OKKA Foundation, 88–97.

Lehmusto, H. 1951. Kasvatusopin historia [The history of didactics]. 2nd (ed.) Porvoo–Helsinki: WSOY.

Lehtonen, K. R. 1983. Valtiovalta ja oppikirjat. Senaatti ja kouluhallitus oppi- ja kansakouluoppikirjojen valvojina Suomessa 1870–1884 [The state and textbooks. Senate and the National Board of Education as monitors of primary school textbooks in Finland 1870–1884]. Research of the Teacher Training Department 9. University of Helsinki.

Leino, A.-L. & Leino, J. 1989. Opettajien ammatillinen kehittyminen [The professional development of teachers]. In: S. Ojanen (Ed.). Akateeminen opettaja [The academic teacher]. University of Helsinki: Lahden tutkimus- ja koulutuskeskus, 15–33.

Lindén, J. 2001. Opettajuus virallisdiskurssissa – myytit, ideaalit ja ammatillinen autonomia [Teacherhood in official discourse – myths, ideals and professional autonomy]. In: E. Ropo (Ed.). Opettajuus ja opetussuunnitelma koulun muutoksessa [Teacherhood and curriculum in school change]. University of Tampere, A 24. Tampere: University Press, 9–32.

Lindqvist, M. 2002. Etiikka ja pahan kohtaaminen kouluyhteisössä [Ethics and facing challenges in a school society]. In: Opetusalan eettinen neuvottelukunta [The ethical advisory board of the teaching profession] & R. Sarras (Eds.). Etiikka koulun arjessa [Ethics in daily school life]. Helsinki: Otava, 75–91.

Lipponen, P. 2003. Kansakouluaate saapuu Kuopion maalaiskuntaan [The primary school ideology arrives in the countryside of Kuopio]. In: J. Rantala (Ed.). Koulu ja kansalaisyhteiskunta historiallisessa perspektiivissä [School and civic society from a historical perspective]. Helsinki: Hakapaino, 62–77.

Loukola, J. L. 1926. Kirjallisuutta [Literature]. Kansakoulun lehti [Journal of Primary school], 20–21.

Luukkainen, O. 2000. Opettaja vuonna 2010 [The teacher in 2010]. Opettajien perus- ja täydennyskoulutuksen ennakointihankeen selvitys 15. Loppuraportti [Report 15 on the preparative project for the basic and supplementary education of teachers. Final report]. Opetushallitus [Board of Education].

Luukkainen, O. 2005. Opettajan matkakirja tulevaan [A teacher's travel guide for the future]. Juva: WS Bookwell Oy.

Lähteenmäki, M. 2000. Vuosisadan naisliike. Naiset ja sosiaalidemokratia 1900 luvun Suomessa [The female movement of the century. Women and social democracy in Finland in the 1900s]. Helsinki: Hakapaino Oy.

MacIntyre, A.1984. After Virtue. A study in moral theory. 2nd (ed.). University of Notre Dame. Indiana: Notre Dame Press.

Manninen, O. 1990. Älkööt aivan monet teistä pyrkikö opettajiksi [I hope not all of you want to become teachers]. In: R. Heikkinen (Ed.). Kasvatusta ja koulutusta korven kaupungissa. Kajaanin opettajankoulutuslaitos 90 vuotta [Schooling and education in the city of woods. The 90th anniversary of the teacher education deprtment of Kajaani]. University of Oulu, 173–178.

Markkola, P. 1994. Työläiskodin synty: tamperelaiset työläisperheet ja yhteiskunnallinen kysymys 1870-luvulta 1910-luvulle [The birth of the worker home: working families in Tampere and the social question from the 1870s–1910s]. Helsinki: SHS [The Finnish Historical Society].

Melin, V. 1980. Alkuopetus Suomen maaseudulla ennen oppivelvollisuuslakia 1866–1921. II Alkuopetuksen liittäminen kunnalliseen oppivelvollisuuskouluun 1906–1921 [Primary education in the Finnish countryside before the Act oncompulsory education 1866–1921. Affiliating primary education into municipal compulsory education 1906–1921]. Acta Universitatis Tamperensis. Ser. A Vol 117. University of Tampere.

Männistö, J. 1994. Sivistyksen kylvö. Suomen kansakoululaitos johtavien puoluelehtien mielenkiinnon kohteena vuosina 1918–1939 [Sowing the seeds of education. The Finnish primary school system as a focus of interest by leading party magazines between 1918–1939]. Acta Universitatis Tamperensis. Ser. A Vol 395. University of Tampere.

Mäntylä, R. 2007. Ammatillinen kasvu ammattikorkeakoulussa [Professional growth in a polytechnic]. In: S. Saari & T. Varis (eds.). Ammatillinen kasvu [Professional growth]. University of Tampere, 92–102

Mäntyoja, A. 1951. Kansakoulun lainsäädäntö [Primary school legislation]. Helsinki: Otava.

Määttä, K.1989. Opettajaksi opiskelleiden kontrolli-ideologia sekä sen muuttuminen opintojen edetessä ja työkokemuksen karttuessa. [The control ideology of teacher training students and its change as studies progressed and experience accumulated]. Educational Publication A 5. University of Lapland.

Niemi, H. 1989. Mitä on opettajan ammatillinen kehittyminen? [What is the professional development of a teacher?]. In: S. Ojanen (Ed.) Akateeminen opettaja [The academic teacher]. University of Helsinki, 66–99.

Niemi, H. 1992. Opettajien ammatillinen kehitys. Osa 1 [Teachers' professional development part 1]. Research of The Faculty of Education 87. University of Oulu.

Niemi, H. 1995. Opettajien ammatillinen kehitys osa 2 [Teachers' professional development part 2]. The Teacher Training Department of University of Tampere A 3.

Niemi, H. 1998. Opettaja modernin murroksessa [The teacher in modern change]. Juva: WSOY.

Niemi, H. & Tirri, K. 1997. Valmiudet opettajan ammattiin opettajien ja opettajien kouluttajien arvioimana [Capabilities for the teaching profession as evaluated by teachers and teacher trainers]. The Teacher Training Department of University of Tampere A 10.

Nurmi, V. 1964. Maamme seminaarien varsinaisen opettajankoulutuksen synty ja kehittyminen viime vuosisadalla I [The genesis and development of our actual teacher education in the last century]. Jyväskylä Studies in Education, Psychology and Social Reasearch 7.

Nurmi, V. 1965. Hyvän opettajan ominaisuuksia [The qualities of a good teacher]. Report of the Department of Education 11. University of Jyväskylä.

Nurmi, V. 1966. Maamme ensimmäisen kansakouluasetuksen synty [The establishment of the first primary school regulation in Finland] In: Kansakoulu 1866–1966 [Primary school 1866–1966]. Helsinki: Otava, 16–20.

Nurmi, V. 1979. Opettajankoulutuksen tähänastinen kehitys [The development of teacher training thus far]. Juva: WSOY.

Nurmi, V. 1981. Maamme koulutusjärjestelmä eilen, tänään, huomenna [Our education system yesterday, today and tomorrow]. Porvoo: WSOY.

Nurmi, V. 1983. Kasvatuksen traditio [The tradition of education]. WSOY: Porvoo.

Nurmi, V. 1988. Uno Cygnaeus. Suomalainen koulumies ja kasvattaja [A Finnish man of school and an educator]. Helsinki: Valtion painatuskeskus.

Nurmi, V. 1989. Kansakoulusta peruskouluun [From the (historical) primary school to the primary school today]. Juva: WSOY.

Nurmi, V. 1995. Suomen kansakouluopettajaseminaarien historia [The history of the primary school teacher colleges of Finland]. Helsinki: OAJ.

Nurmi, V. 1996. Opettajankoulutusta Raumalla 100 vuotta [Teacher training in Rauma for 100 years]. The Faculty of Education A 176. University of Turku.

Ojakangas, M. 2003. J. V. Snellman ja kansallinen kasvatus [J.V. Snellman and national education]. In: J. Rantala (Ed.). Koulu ja kansalaisyhteiskunta historiallisessa perspektiivissä [School and society from a historical perspective]. Helsinki: Hakapaino, 47–61.

OPM 2001. Opettajankoulutuksen kehittämisohjelma – Utvecklingprogram för lärarutbildningen [Teacher training development programme]. Opetusministeriö [Ministry of Education]. Helsinki.

OPM 2008:9. Koulutus ja tutkimus 2007–2012. Kehittämissuunnitelma [Education and research 2007–2012. Development plan]. Opetusministeriö [Ministry of Education]. Publications 2008:9. Helsinki: University Press.

Ottelin, A. K.1931. Kasvatusopin pääpiirteet I [The main features of pedagogy I]. Yleinen kasvatusoppi [General pedagogy]. Helsinki: Otava

Palmén, A. & Wilksman, I.1921. Terveysoppi. Kouluja varten [Hygiene for schools]. Helsinki: Otava.

Paksuniemi, M. 2009. Tornion alakansakoulunopettajaseminaarin opettajakuva lukuvuosina 1921–1945 rajautuen oppilasvalintoihin, oppikirjoihin ja oheistoimintaan [The teacher image at lower primary school teacher training college of Tornio during 1921–1945 focusing on student admission, textbooks and supplementary activities]. Rovaniemi: University of Lapland.

Peltonen, M. 1989. Jyväskylän kansakoulun historia [The history of primary school in Jyväskylä]. Jyväskylä.

Perho, H. 1982. Ammatti- ja opintosuuntautumisen luonne ja merkitys luokanopettajan opinnoissa [The nature and significance of vocational study orientation in class teacher education]. Publication of the Univeristy of Joensuu A 23.

Petterson, L. 1992. Frihet, jämlikhet, egendom och Bentham. Utvecklingslinjer i svensk folkundervisning mellan feodalism och kapitalism 1809–1860 [Freedom, equality, property and Bentham. Educational trends in Swedish school system between feodalism and capitalism in 1809–1860]. Acta universitatis Upsaliensis. Studia Historica Upsaliensia 168. University of Uppsala.

Pickle, J. 1985. Toward Teacher Maturity. Journal of Teacher Education, 4, 55–59.

Pietarinen, J. & Poutanen, S. 1998. Etiikan teorioita [Theries of ethics]. Gaudeamus. Tampere: Tammer-Paino Oy.

Pietilä, A. J. 1928. Kristillinen siveysoppi kansakoulun opettajaseminaareja varten [Christian decency education for elementary school teacher training colleges], Helsinki: Osakeyhtiö Valistus.

Pursiainen, T. 2002. Ammattien etiikka [The ethics of occupations]. In: Opetusalan eettinen neuvottelukunta [The ethical advisory board of the teaching profession] & R. Sarras (Eds.). Etiikka koulun arjessa [Ethics in daily school life]. Helsinki: Otava, 35–53.

Pyysiäinen, M. 1994. Uuden päivän alku. Päivänavauskäytäntö peruskoulussa ja lukiossa sekä opettajien käsitykset päivänavauksesta [The beginning of the new day. Morning assemblies in primary schools and high school, and the teachers'opinions of them]. Publication of The Department of Practical Theology 78. Helsinki: Kirkkohallitus.

Rantala, J. 2002. Kansakoulunopettajat ja kapina. Vuoden punaisuussyytökset ja opettajan asema paikallisyhteisössä [Primary school teachers and rebellion. The accusations of the year for being a communist and the teachers position in the local community]. Historical Research 214. Helsinki: Finnish Literature Society.

Rantala, J. 2005. Kansaa kasvattamassa [Educating people]. Jyväskylä: Gummerrus.
Renvall, P. 1965. Nykyajan historiantutkimus [Modern research of history]. Helsinki: WSOY.
Rinne, M. 1973. Suomen Opettajain Liitto 1893–1973 [The association of Finland's teachers in 1893–1973]. Vammala: Vammalan Kirjapaino Oy.
Rinne, R.1986a. Kansanopettaja mallikansalaisena: Opettajuuden laajeneminen ja opettajuuden rekrytoimismekanismit Suomessa 1851–1986 virallisen kuvausaineiston ilmaisemana [The teacher as a model citizen: The expansion of the teacher profession and recruitment methods in Finland in 1851–1988 illustrated by official data]. The Publication of the Faculty of Education A 108. University of Turku.
Rinne, R. 1986b. Kansakoulunopettajien rekrytointi Suomessa ennen toista maailmansotaa [Recruitment of primary school teachers in Finland before the Second World War]. In: Koulu ja menneisyys [School and the past]. Finnish Historical School Society yearbook. Helsinki: University Press, 128–158.
Rinne, R.1989. Mistä opettajat tulevat? Suomalaisen kansanopettajiston yhteiskunnallinen tausta sekä kulttuurinen ja sosiaalinen pääoma 1800-luvun puolivälistä 1980-luvun lopulle [Where are teachers from? The societal background and social capital of Finnish teachers from the middle of the 1800s to the end of the 1980s]. Turku: University of Turku.
Rinne, R. & Jauhiainen, A.1988. Koulutus, professionaalistuminen ja valtio. Julkisen sektorin koulutettujen reproduktioammattikuntien muotoutuminen Suomessa [Education, becoming a professional and the state. The formation of educated reproduction professions in the public sector in Finland]. The Publication of the Faculty of Education A 128. University of Turku.
Ropo, E. & Huopainen, M. 2001. Koulu opetussuunnitelma uudistuksen pyörteissä: Havaintoja opettajien ja rehtoreiden kokemuksista opetussuunnitelmaprosessin vaiheista peruskoulussa [The school curriculum amid reform: Observations on teachers' and principals' experiences of the stages of the curriculum process in primary schools]. In: E. Ropo

(Ed.). Opettajuus ja opetussuunnitelma koulun muutoksessa [Teacherhood and the curriculum during school change]. University of Tampere A 24. Tampere: University Press, 33–46.

Räihä, P. 2010. Koskaan et muuttua saa! Luokanopettajakoulutuksen opiskelijavalintojen uudistamisen vaikeudesta [You can't ever change! On the difficulty of reforming class teacher training student selection]. Acta Universitatis Tamperiensis 1559. University of Tampere.

Salmela, A. 1931. Etiikan alkeet. Oppikirja seminaareja ja yksinopiskelijoita varten [The basics of ethics. A textbook for colleges and independent students]. Porvoo: WSOY.

Salmela, A. 1935. Suomen kansakouluhallinnon pääpiirteet [The main features of the Finnish primary school administration]. Porvoo: WSOY.

Salo. A. 1919. Ensimmäisen ja toisen kouluvuoden lukemisen opetus I. Alkeiden opetus [Teaching reading for the first and second grade 1. Teaching the basics]. Helsinki: Otava.

Salo. A. 1924. Kasvatusopillisen sielutieteen pääpiirteet. Oppikirja opettajain valmistuslaitoksia varten [The main features of educational psychology. A textbook for teacher education colleges]. Helsinki: Otava.

Salo. A. 1926. Alakansakoulun opetusoppi I. Yleiset opetusopilliset suuntaviivat [Didactics of the primary school I. General didactical guidelines]. Helsinki: Otava.

Salo. A. 1928. Alakansakoulun opetusoppi II. Ympäristöopetus. [Didactics of the primary school. Environmental studies]. Helsinki: Otava.

Salo. A. 1929. Alakansakoulun opetusoppi IV. Puhumisen ja lukemisen opetus [Didactics of the primary school. Teaching speaking and reading]. Helsinki: Otava.

Salo, A. 1934. Alakansakoulun opetusoppi II [Didactics of the primary school II]. Helsinki: Otava.

Salo. A. 1935. Uusi Aapinen [The New ABC book]. Helsinki: Otava.

Salo. A. 1944. Ulkomaiden kansa- ja oppikoulujen rakenne [The stucture of primary schools abroad]. Alakansakoulu [Lower Primary School] 24, 371–372.

Simola, H.1995. Paljon vartijat. Suomalainen kansanopettaja valtiollisessa kouludiskurssissa 1860-luvulta 1990-luvulle [Many responsibilities:

the Finnish folk teacher in the national educational discourse from the 1860s to the 1990s]. The Teacher Training Department 137. University of Helsinki.

Sipilä, P. 1998. Sukupuolitettu ihminen – kokonainen etiikka. Onko sukupuoli oikein? [The gendered person – comprehensive ethics. Is gender correct?]. Gaudeamus. Tampere: Tammer-Paino Oy.

Soininen, M. 1911. Lyhyt kasvatus- ja opetusoppi [Short didactics and pedagogy]. Helsinki: Otava.

Soininen, M. 1923. Yleinen kasvatusoppi [General didactics]. (4th Eds.) Helsinki: Otava.

Somerkivi, U. 1979. Kouluhallitus ja koulutoimen kehittyminen satavuotiskautena 1869–1969 [The development of the National Board of Education and the school system over a period of a century 1869–1969]. In: U. Somerkivi, G. Cavonius & M. O. Karttunen. Kouluhallitus. Skolstyrelesen 1869–1969. [The National Board of Education 1869–1969]. Vantaa: Kunnallispaino, 11–128.

Stenroth, F. 1923. Kansakoulun voimistelua [Gymnastics at the primary school]. Helsinki: Otava.

Stenroth, F. 1929. Kansakoulun voimistelua [Gymnastics at the primary school]. Helsinki: Otava.

Stormbom, J. 1991. Ketkä olivat Suomen didaktisesti merkittävimmät herbartilaiset ja mitä oli didaktiikka? [Who were the most important herbartians of the didactics in Finland and what was didactics?]. Finnish Historical School Society yearbook. Helsinki: University Press, 119–131.

Syrjäläinen, E.1995. Koulukohtaisen opetussuunnitelman toteutuminen: opettajan ansa vai mahdollisuus? [The school-specific implementation of the curriculum: a teacher trap or opportunity?]. The Teacher Training Department A 5. University of Tampere.

Syrjäläinen, E. 1997. Arvioinnin avulla laatua kouluihin. -Markkinahumua vai koulurealismia?[Quality in schools through evaluation – Marketing pitch or school realism?]. The Teacher Training Department A 11. University of Tampere.

Syrjäläinen, E. 2002. Eikö opettaja saisi jo opettaa? Koulun kehittämisen paradoksi ja opettajan työuupumus [Can't a teacher just teach already? The paradox of school development and teacher burnout]. The Teacher Training Department A 25. University of Tampere.

Syrjäläinen, E. 2009. Tuottavuutta, mutta millä hinnalla? Opettajat kehittämisen kehässä [Productivity, but at what price? Teachers in a cycle of development]. In: K. Kurtakko, J. Leinonen & M. Pehkonen (Eds.). Opettajaksi kehittyminen, hyvinvointi ja oppimisen strategiat [Becoming a teacher, strategies for wellbeing and learning]. Rovaniemi: University Press, 140–154.

Syväoja, H. 2004. Kansakoulu –suomalaisten kasvattaja. Perussivistystä koko kansalle 1866–1977 [The primary school –the educator of Finnish people. Basic education for the whole nation 1866–1977]. Juva: WS Bookwell Oy.

Säntti, J. 2003. Muuttuva opettajuus sotienjälkeisessä Suomessa [Changing teacherhood after the war years in Finland]. In: J. Rantala (Ed.). Koulu ja kansalaisyhteiskunta historiallisessa perspektiivissä. [School and civic society from a historical perspective]. Helsinki, 172–198.

Takala, A.1997. Ihmiseksi kasvaminen [Growing into a human]. Helsinki: Gummerrus.

Tamminen, K. 1998. Suomalaisen uskonnon didaktiikan kehityslinjoja [The developmental trends of Finnish didactics of RE]. In: M, Pyysiäinen & K. Tamminen (Eds.). Uskonnonopetuksen käsikirja [A handbook for religious education]. Juva: WSOY, 15–40.

Tirri, K.1996.Teachers'professional morality: How teacher education prepares teacher to identify and solve moral dilemmas at school. In H. Niemi & K. Tirri (Eds.). Effectiveness of Teacher Education. New Challanges and Approaches to Evaluation. The Teacher Training Department A 6. University of Tampere, 83–94.

Tirri, K. 1999a. Eettisten kysymysten äärellä [Near ethical questions]. In: H. Niemi (Ed.). Opettajankoulutus modernin murroksessa [Teacher training in modern change]. Tampere: University Press, 150–167.

Tirri, K. 1999b. Opettajan ammattietiikka [The professional ethics of a teacher]. Juva: WSOY.

Tirri, K. 2002. Opetustyön keskeiset eettiset ongelmakohdat. Teoksessa: Opetusalan eettinen neuvottelukunta [The ethical advisory board of the teaching profession] & R. Sarras (Eds.). Etiikka koulun arjessa [Ethics in daily school life]. Helsinki: Otava, 23–32.

Tuomaala, S. 2004. Työtätekevistä käsistä puhtaiksi ja kirjoittaviksi. Suomalaisen oppivelvollisuuskoulun ja maalaisten kohtaaminen 1921–1939. [The transformation from workers hands to writers clean hands. Finnish compulsory education and rural society meet in 1921–1939]. Helsinki: Hakapaino Oy. SKS [The Finnish Literature Society].

Tupper, K. W. 2008. Teaching teacher to just say "know": Reflections on drug education, Teaching and Teacher Education, 24, 356–367.

Tuunainen, K. & Nevala, A. 1986. Erityiskasvatus koko ikäluokan kasvatuksen osana. Erityiskasvatuksen historiallisen kehityksen piirteitä Suomessa 1860-luvulta peruskoulun tuloon [Special education as part of the education of the entire age group. Features of the historical development of special education in Finland from the 1860s until the arrival of primary school]. Research of the Faculty of Education 14. University of Joensuu.

Törnudd, L.1929. Uusi käsitöiden oppikirja [A new textbook for handicrafts]. 5th (ed.) Jyväskylä: Gummerus.

Uusikylä, K. 2002. Rohkeus ja välittäminen. -Opettajan moraalin peruspilarit [Courage and caring – the pillars of teacher morals]. In: Opetusalan eettinen neuvottelukunta [The ethical advisory board of the teaching profession] & R. Sarras (Eds.). Etiikka koulun arjessa [Ethics in daily school life]. Helsinki: Otava, 9–21.

Wallin, O.1893. Yleinen kasvatus- ja opetusoppi [General didactics and pedagogy]. 2nd (ed.) Gummerrus: Jyväskylä.

Valta, J. 2002. Ongelmaoppilaat Oulun kansakoulussa vuosina 1874–1974 [Difficult pupils in primary schools of Oulu]. Faculty of Education E 54. University of Oulu.

Valve, T. & Tappura, K. 1937. Kansakoulun käsityöt [Handicraft for primary school]. 3rd (ed.). Porvoo: WSOY.

Vartia, A. 1931. Kouluhygienia [School hygiene]. 2nd (ed.) Helsinki: Otava.

Virta, I. 2001. Siirtoväen kansakoulukysymys sotavuosien Suomessa. [The question of primary school and displaced population in Finland during the war years]. University of Turku C 169. Turku: Painosalama Oy.

Virrankoski, P. 1975. Suomen taloushistoria kivikaudesta atomiaikaan [The economic history of Finland from the stone age to nuclear age]. Helsinki: Otava.

Vonk, J. H. C. & Schras, G. A. 1987. From beginning to experienced teacher: A Study of the professional development of teachers during their first four years of service. European Journal of Teacher Education 10, 95–110.

Värri, V.-M. 2001. Mallikansalaisesta psykokapitalismin muutosagentiksi. Aikalaiskriittinen tarina opettajan identiteetin hajoamisesta [From model citizen to a psychocapitalist agent for change. A contemporary critical story of the break down of the teacher identity]. In: E. Ropo (Ed.). Opettajuus ja opetussuunnitelma koulun muutoksessa [Teacherhood and the curriculum during school change]. University of Tampere A 24. Tampere: University Press 33–46.

Värri, V.-M. 2002. Opettaja tässä ajassa [The teacher at the present time]. -Viisi teesiä opettajan etiikasta [Five theses on teacher ethics]. In: Opetusalan eettinen neuvottelukunta [The ethical advisory board of the teaching profession] & R. Sarras (Eds.). Etiikka koulun arjessa [Ethics in daily school life]. Helsinki: Otava, 55–63.

Ziller, T.1857. Die Regierung der Kinder. Für gebildete Eltern, Lehrer und Studierende [Controlling a Child]. Leipzig: Teubner.

Ziller, T.1876. Vorlesungen über allgemeine Pädagogik. [General Pedagogy]. Leipzig: Matthes.

www.ingramcontent.com/pod-product-compliance
Ingram Content Group UK Ltd.
Pitfield, Milton Keynes, MK11 3LW, UK
UKHW041438190426
11946UKWH00021B/17